The Business Owner's Definitive Guide to

CAPTIVE INSURANCE COMPANIES

The Business Owner's Definitive Guide to

CAPTIVE INSURANCE COMPANIES

*What you need to know about **formation** and **management***

Peter J. Strauss, J.D., LL.M.

The Strauss Law Firm, LLC

Hamilton Captive Management, LLC

ForbesBooks

Published by ForbesBooks, Charleston, South Carolina.
Member of Advantage Media Group.

ForbesBooks is a registered trademark, and the ForbesBooks colophon is a trademark of Forbes Media, LLC.

Printed in the United States of America.

10 9 8 7 6 5 4 3 2 1

ISBN: 978-1-94663-307-1
LCCN: 2017941933

Cover and layout design by George Stevens.

TABLE OF CONTENTS

Meet the Author

Peter J. Strauss is the managing member of The Strauss Law Firm, LLC, located on Hilton Head Island, South Carolina. His firm is devoted to providing estate and tax planning, asset protection, international business, and captive insurance solutions to individuals, families, and business owners located both in the United States and internationally.

Mr. Strauss is also the founder and CEO of Hamilton Captive Management, LLC, the largest captive management firm licensed in the Bahamas, as well as numerous insurance companies, including Worldwide Property & Casualty Ltd., SAC, and Madison First Property & Casualty Ltd., SAC, segregated accounts companies responsible for ongoing compliance, governance, and reporting requirements for clients in over forty states; and Port Royal Insurance Company Ltd., SAC, the only licensed reinsurance provider in the Bahamas.

Mr. Strauss has authored several books on captive insurance, including *Captive Insurance Companies for the Small Business Owner*, *The Definitive Guide to Captive Insurance Companies,* and *The Physician's Guide to Captive Insurance Companies.* He regularly speaks at public seminars and professional society meetings, such as the American Institute of Certified Public Accountants (AICPA), Hawaii

Tax Institute (HTI), Southern Federal Tax Institute (SFTI), and Continuing Legal Education (CLE) conferences.

Mr. Strauss is a graduate of the New England School of Law, and he holds an LL.M. in estate planning from the University of Miami. In 2016, he was accepted to Harvard Business School Executive Education's Owner/President Management (OPM) program and recently completed Unit I of an intensive three-unit format that takes place over three years onsite at Harvard Business School. Each unit is designed to expand expertise in eight key areas—strategy, finance, marketing, negotiations, global markets, leadership, entrepreneurship, and operations and technology.

The unique program provides forward-looking business owners and entrepreneurs with the skills, tools, and networks to address the unique challenges their companies face and become more effective leaders. Upon completion of OPM, Mr. Strauss will be granted full HBS alumni status and gain exclusive access to the vast global alumni network and an array of resources that facilitate lifelong learning, growth, and success.

Additionally, Mr. Strauss lives on Hilton Head Island, South Carolina, with his wife, Mackenzie, and their four children, Colin, Quinn, Rymer, and Penny.

Acknowledgments

I must begin by thanking my wife, Mackenzie, and my four children—Colin, Quinn, Rymer, and Penny—who inspire me every day and offer unwavering support. Mackenzie, each and every day brings something special. Thank you for letting me be me and embracing the chaos! To my parents, what can I say other than "What a ride!" Pato, everyone should be so lucky as to have a friend like you. I'm fortunate enough to call you a brother! Sorry Ted, I love you too!

I would also like to thank my teams at The Strauss Law Firm, LLC, and Hamilton Captive Management, LLC, for their patience and assistance in publishing this book, as well as their support on a daily basis. It was just an idea! Let's continue to change each other's lives together! Joe Z, why be boring, right? Good days, bad days—all good when you are challenged each and every day with making something special. Gresh, Birdie, you walk, I walk! Nate, thank you for letting me sit right seat!

Writing a book is a journey on so many levels. Even what ultimately becomes "just a revision" is in and of itself just that, a journey. It could be argued that revising a book is more difficult than starting from scratch. This book required a level of introspection far different than any of my other projects. I spent countless hours peeling back the layers of past words, descriptions, concepts, and decisions. Oftentimes it required acknowledging my own flaws or recognizing better choices that could have been made.

Special thanks to each and every client I have and continue to work with. I learn so much more from you than I could ever possibly teach. I'm grateful for the opportunity to work with each and every one of you! Beller, never a dull moment, never a bad time. Thank you, brother. To my team at Harvard—Risso, Aung, Vivek, Nitin, Rajesh, and Lai—the journey continues! To my T21 guys in Miami, Dallas, and, of course, Austin, words can't describe the purposeful impact you have had and continue to have. There are so many of you I'd love to mention by name but I think you know exactly who you are!

—Peter J. Strauss

Preface

When I set out to write my first book on captive insurance, I did so without understanding the world of publishing. In fact, I stumbled across the topic of captive insurance by accident. A client asked me to assist in establishing a captive, and I actually advised them not to form a captive insurance company because it seemed too good to be true. I wrote the first book as a research project to better understand captive insurance companies for myself and in turn to educate clients and advisors.

After the book was published and, shortly thereafter, started selling online at various retailers, my life changed forever. Countless speeches, more airplane flights than I care to remember, and now a concept that has grown so popular that the federal government has recently amended the Internal Revenue Code to increase the scope and capabilities for captive owners. This is what I refer to as my "accidental life"! Not knowing anything about publishing, and not understanding how popular the topic of captive insurance would be with business owners, was just the beginning.

As the popularity of captive insurance companies has grown, so too has my understanding of the incredible power and flexibility of the insurance industry as a whole. When the Internal Revenue Code was amended on January 1, 2017, it forced me to revisit my previous writings and not just revise the code section contained within the book but also face some truths about my practice in that we've evolved as a practice and found stronger, more concrete methods in developing and implementing captive insurance companies. In doing so, I've been forced to revisit the message being sent by my books and articles. What started as a remodel turned into a fairly significant renovation as I recognized that not only has the industry evolved but so have I.

When the first three books were written, my practice focused on the establishment of captives, not on their management. For each captive insurance company formed, we would outsource its management to third-party independent managers. After several years, it became apparent that while proper coordination and implementation of a captive were fundamental, so too were the ongoing operations, compliance, regulatory and corporate governance and, of course, legal oversight. Hamilton Captive Management was born with the understanding that the management of captives is just as important as their establishment. While I never intended to operate a management company alongside a law firm, the decision was made out of necessity.

With the establishment of Hamilton, we were now armed with operational knowledge and experience. After some growing pains, lessons learned, and an absolute focus on being the best each and every day, it turns out that there is a difference between just forming a captive insurance company and forming a captive insurance company the right way—and that much of what I was taught, told, and led to believe wasn't correct. It is with this "truth" that I offer you this book. The previously written books, although perhaps fundamentally correct, only told a version of the story. I believe this book more accurately delivers a message and reflects the appropriate way to plan and establish a captive.

Chapter One
FUNDAMENTAL PRINCIPLES

What You Need to Know about Captive Insurance

Life is filled with risk. Every day, you take risks in your business. Some of these risks are calculated—after all, you must take on some risk in order to make a profit in your business. Other risks may not be so well known to you or may not usually be at the forefront of your mind. For example, you may carry insurance on the truck used to make deliveries in your business, but you may not think to carry similar insurance on the computer used to track your deliveries or inventory. There may be other risks that you know about but that are simply too expensive for you to insure or that you didn't know insurance was available for.

To further compound the issue, there is no tax benefit to self-insurance—there is no tax deduction unless you pay an insurance company a premium to insure your business against these risks. According to the American Institute of Certified Public Accountants

(AICPA), most businesses unknowingly self-insure a great part of their risks from daily business activities. More specifically stated:

> *Self-insurance, whether funded out of company reserves or personal after-tax savings, is not tax-deductible. To compound the problem, smaller deductibles are expensive and not tax beneficial.*

The solution, according to this AICPA report, is a captive insurance company. Properly structured, "self-insurance through a captive structure can create substantial tax deductions, resulting in tremendous tax savings."

Captive insurance produces material tax savings that help you to save real dollars in your business. Furthermore, captive insurance helps businesses address the problem of inadequate insurance that traditionally has been unavailable or too expensive on the commercial market. And yet, most business owners have no idea what captive insurance is, much less how to use it to their advantage.

Captive insurance is a strategy whereby your business purchases insurance coverage from an insurance company that you own and control (i.e., a "captive" insurance company). The premiums paid by your business are tax deductible. Meanwhile, the premiums that your captive collects are tax-free. You read that correctly: the premiums collected by your captive insurance company are tax-free.

Suppose your business pays $1 million in premiums to your captive insurance company every year. Assume further that your combined federal and state income tax rate is 50 percent. Your business would deduct $1 million from its taxable income, saving you $500,000 *each year*. Furthermore, that $1 million would be received free of income tax *each year* inside your captive insurance company. You would pay less in taxes, have a more robust risk management tool, and have more money in the bank.

In this first chapter, I will start you out with a brief history of captive insurance, sharing with you how captive insurance came to evolve into an insurance strategy with tremendous tax savings potential. I will then provide you with an overview of the fundamental legal and tax principles governing captive insurance planning. Finally, I will walk you through an overview of the captive insurance industry so that you have a better understanding of how captive insurance works and how captive insurance companies operate to provide better coverage, more strategically finance their risk management, and potentially save their owners money. By the end of this chapter, you should have a basic understanding of what captive insurance is and how it works. More importantly, you should gain some insight into the cost savings, risk management, and potential tax savings involved in utilizing captive insurance in your business.

A Brief History Of Captive Insurance

To help you better understand how captive insurance works, I would first like to walk you through its origins. It all began with a company in Youngstown, Ohio, called Youngstown Sheet and Tube Company and their insurance agent, a man by the name of Fred Reiss.

The City of Youngstown and the Steel Industry

Youngstown is a rough-and-tumble Rust Belt city on the Mahoning River, almost in a straight line halfway between Cleveland to the northwest and Pittsburgh to the southeast. The city first earned a reputation for its large coal deposits. With the discovery of iron ore nearby, Youngstown also became a center for steel production. At the turn of the twentieth century, as large national steel companies were making their way into Youngstown, a group of local businessmen founded the Youngstown Sheet and Tube Company. At the same time, labor unions were beginning to make inroads into the Youngstown steel factories.

Youngstown Sheet and Tube gradually earned a reputation for not being easy to intimidate. In 1916, workers at the company went on strike, setting fire to a portion of the city, and afterward East Youngstown was renamed the City of Campbell in honor of the company's president, who stood up against the strikers. In 1937, unions banded together and staged what became known as the Little Steel Strike. Youngstown Sheet and Tube joined a group of steel mills that resisted signing an agreement with the strikers.

The Steel Seizure Case

Later, in the early 1950s, labor unions again confronted Youngstown Sheet and Tube, pressing for wage increases during the Korean War. As steel mills were under government-imposed price controls, the management at Youngstown Sheet and Tube refused to give into the strikers' demands. When the unions sought help from a labor-friendly White House, in 1952 President Truman issued an executive order seizing Youngstown Sheet and Tube's steel mills. The company's lawyers immediately went to court to fight the presidential decree as unlawful.

The resulting US Supreme Court decision in *Youngstown Sheet & Tube Co. v. Sawyer*[1] became known as the "Steel Seizure Case" and was a rebuke of the US president's authority. The Supreme Court ruled

1 | 343 US 579 (1952)

that the president could not seize private property without specific authorization in the Constitution or under an act of Congress.

Fred Reiss, the Inventor of Captive Insurance

Around the time that Youngstown Sheet and Tube was fighting President Truman over the right to control its own destiny, Frederic Mylett Reiss entered the picture. Reiss had served in the navy and gone through college on the GI Bill. After college, he went to work for the Ohio Inspection Bureau, assessing insurance risks for large plants and steel mills.

Working next as an underwriter in Cleveland, Reiss became familiar with the techniques for calculating premiums and drafting reinsurance agreements. Finally, he accepted a position with an insurance agency in Youngstown, where he sought to put his talents to good use.

Reiss began working with Youngstown Sheet and Tube, helping them to procure insurance for their steel mills. At that time, most of the policies for large factories and steel mills were underwritten among a handful of large insurance companies. There was a limited supply of available insurers, and premiums were skyrocketing. When Youngstown Sheet and Tube, one of Reiss's largest clients, saw its financial stability threatened by rising insurance prices, Reiss decided to call on his colleagues in London and take action.

The Captive Insurance Solution

Reiss developed a creative solution for his client, Youngstown Sheet and Tube, with the help of Lloyd's insurance underwriters in London. Instead of paying hefty premiums to buy insurance from a large insurance company, Reiss's client would form a new insurance company in Ohio, Steel Insurance Company of America. Steel Insurance would issue insurance to its parent company, Youngstown Sheet and Tube.

Lloyd's of London helped out by providing reinsurance to Steel Insurance. If a large claim hit the newfound insurance company, Lloyd's would be able to pay on the claim, protecting Youngstown Sheet and Tube financially from a catastrophic claim. At the same time, Steel Insurance would be responsible for processing its own claims and paying on smaller claims.

It's All in the Name

Youngstown Sheet and Tube owned a number of coke and iron mines that supplied its steel mills, guaranteeing a supply of raw materials free from external market forces. These mines were known among the company's executives as "captive mines." When Reiss set out to form Steel Insurance for Youngstown Sheet and Tube in 1955, he labeled the insurance subsidiary a "captive" insurance carrier.

Captive Insurance Moves Offshore

As if creating the first captive insurance company was not enough, Reiss also created the first captive management company, International Risk Management Limited, in Bermuda in 1962. Bermuda has since become world renowned for its captive insurance industry, although many other countries also host vibrant captive insurance markets. Many US states have also jumped into the game, enacting business-friendly captive insurance laws that permit you to do everything here in the United States.

Captive Insurance in a Nutshell

What Is Captive Insurance?

From the preceding discussion, you may have gathered that when Youngstown Sheet and Tube set up its own insurance company, Steel Insurance, and bought a policy from Steel Insurance, Youngstown Sheet and Tube was basically insuring itself. In fact, *captive insurance is a form of self-insurance,* although it is not entirely self-insurance; Steel Insurance, for example, ended up reinsuring most of its risks with Lloyd's of London.

Smart business owners engage in self-insurance almost every day in their businesses. You may have declined one or another form of coverage offered to you by your insurance agent in the past, and when you did so, you were making a conscious choice: you would prefer to live with the risk (and suffer the consequences of not being insured) than to pay money for insurance. That is what is known as self-insurance.

Consider for a moment the number of people who drive without basic auto insurance. This is an example of self-insurance by choice, but what if you have no choice? What if insurance simply is not available? Many business owners find themselves in this position, unable to obtain certain forms of coverage because it is too expensive or unavailable on the commercial market.

If captive insurance is not unlike self-insurance, then why would you need a captive insurance company? I will explain the benefits of captive insurance to you in a moment. However, bear in mind this one point: captive insurance is a way of quantifying the amount by which you self-insure.

Let me explain this with a simple example. Assume you have a commercial liability insurance policy for your business each year, and that policy costs $25,000. If you pay the premium for that year, you deduct $25,000 from the revenue (and taxable income) of your business. If, however, you choose not to pay the premium, there's no deduction. Even though you are choosing to self-insure for coverage that is worth $25,000, there is no physical payment of $25,000 that you can claim on your business tax return.

The lesson to draw from this example is that *you cannot deduct the value of risks you self-insure in your business each year. However, by using a captive insurance company, you can deduct the premiums paid, even on risks that might be self-insured.*

What Is a Captive Insurance Company?

A captive insurance company is nothing more than an insurance company that you (or your business) owns. Fred Reiss borrowed the name from the "captive" mines that Youngstown Sheet and Tube owned and used to supply raw materials for their steel mills. A captive insurance company is one that is related to the business that it insures.

You should note that we are talking about a captive *insurance company*. I am not referring to a shell company that is formed by filing a simple set of papers with your local secretary of state's office. This is an actual insurance company that is formed and licensed for the specific purpose of providing real insurance coverage to your business. Likewise, it is operated as an insurance company, with real insurance policies, a service office, claims processing, reinsurance, and more.

The Design of the Captive Insurance Plan

As you may gather from the historical overview of captive insurance, Reiss's original design was pretty simple:

- An operating business forms its own insurance company;
- the insurance company provides insurance to the operating business;
- the insurance company acquires reinsurance coverage to protect against catastrophic claims; and
- the insurance company processes its own claims and pays out of its own pocket for smaller claims, using reinsurance to handle bigger claims.

That's it. That is all you need to know. Sounds simple, doesn't it? Of course, everything is in the details (and in chapter 3 I will dive into detail on how each of these four design points works), but I want you to understand this point: *captive insurance is a simple concept.* Just as you know how to run your business even if you don't understand how to run every machine in your factory, if you keep these four design points in mind you will know how to examine a captive insurance structure—even if you are not ready to start writing your own policy forms and processing your own claims.

Benefits of Captive Insurance: What's in It for Me?

Fred Reiss formed Steel Insurance for his client because steel mills in the 1950s were having difficulty buying insurance in the face of skyrocketing premiums. Depending on the business you are in, particularly if you are in a high-risk occupation (such as manufacturing) or have lots of employees, you too may be facing skyrocketing premiums. Captive insurance might be a way for you to take control of ever-rising premiums. After all, if you pay a lot in premiums to an outside insurance company and don't make any claims, that money is lost for all time. If instead you pay premiums to your own captive, the profits from a low claims history are yours to keep inside your captive.

Another benefit of captive insurance is tax related. As you may know, the US tax law, called the Internal Revenue Code of 1986 (IRC), is riddled with loopholes and exclusions. I am not about to editorialize on US tax policy, but I do want you to be aware of a phenomenal tax benefit that is there for the taking. Nobody is going to just give it to you; you have to make the effort to claim it. To best understand this, let's start with an example:

> James is a successful dental surgeon, having built Tidewater Dental from a single office with three employees to a multi-state practice with forty employees and three locations. The company grosses $5 million annually.
>
> Tidewater Dental is an S corporation; all net income flows through to James on his personal tax return. James pays a top combined federal and state income tax rate of approximately 50 percent.
>
> James meets with his attorney and decides to form a captive insurance company. His new company, Tidewater Insurance, insures commercial liability and property used in his business. In the first year of this new captive insurance arrangement, Tidewater Dental pays $300,000 in premiums to Tidewater Insurance.

Whenever you pay an insurance premium in your business for commercial liability and property coverage, it is normally an expense of the business that is deducted against income. Therefore, in this example, James deducts $300,000 against his S corporation income for the premium paid into Tidewater Insurance. *Since James is taxed at a 50 percent rate, deducting $300,000 from his business income saves him $150,000 in taxes.*

"Wait a minute," you may say to yourself. "What happens to that $300,000?" The premium is paid into James's own captive insurance company. Now, insurance companies are taxed like any other company; they pay taxes on their income. *However, there is a little-known provision of the US tax law that exempts the first $2.2 million of premium income in a captive insurance company* (this will be further discussed momentarily). When Tidewater Dental pays $300,000 into Tidewater Insurance, the insurance company receives this money *free of income tax.*

It gets better. The $2.2 million exclusion (which is also indexed for inflation) that Congress bestows on "small" insurance companies is an *annual* exclusion: you get to exempt up to $2.2 million (again, indexed for inflation) *each year* from the captive's premium income. In this example, James could keep paying $300,000 each year into his captive, continuing to rack up greater and greater tax savings provided the claims are managed appropriately.

It doesn't end there. There are additional tax benefits available to captives that I don't want to get into just yet. However, if you run the example of James paying $300,000 in premiums every year to his own captive, and you allow for reasonable dividends and capital growth on the investment portfolio inside the captive, James's portfolio would hold just under $4 million after ten years. *This is money that would otherwise go to taxes; it would not exist if James did not use a captive.*

I want you to grasp the following principles from this part of the discussion:

1. Captive insurance offers important tax benefits.
2. These tax benefits are not available unless you have a captive insurance company.

Why Have I Not Heard of This Before?

This is perhaps the most commonly asked question. The provision of the tax law that provides this valuable benefit is IRC § 831(b), commonly known as the "small insurance company exclusion." In fact, captives that claim this benefit are frequently referred to in the industry as "831(b) captives." When you look at the history of captive insurance, some of which has already been discussed in this book, it is surprising that more business owners haven't already heard of it. With that being said, over the past several years the momentum in the business community is certainly there. There are now thousands of captive insurance companies and over eighty licensed domiciles worldwide in which to establish your captive insurance company!

Further, the momentum is such that on December 18, 2015, the Protecting Americans from Tax Hikes Act of 2015 (hereinafter, The PATH Act) was signed into law, amending § 831(b) in two ways. First, it increased the maximum amount of premium an insurance company may receive annually while still remaining eligible to make the 831(b) election—from $1.2 million to $2.2 million (effective January 1, 2017). The limit is indexed for inflation.

Second, it added a diversification requirement that can be satisfied in one of two ways. The first, known as the "risk diversification test," is met if no more than 20 percent of net written premium is received by the insurance company from a single policyholder. If the insurance company does not meet this requirement, the second test is the "relatedness test." The relatedness test, which applies to spouses and lineal descendants, requires that owners of the insured business must own a share of the business equal to or greater than their ownership in the captive. We will discuss this topic later in the book.

Is This Legal?

If "Why have I not heard of this before?" is the most commonly asked question, perhaps "Is this legal?" is the second most commonly asked question. The short answer is "*Yes.*" The longer answer is that not only is captive insurance perfectly legal, but also consider this: Out of all the deductions your business claims on its tax return each year, how many are based on a risk management strategy with its own Internal Revenue Code section and decades of case law, revenue rulings, and revenue procedures? Not many. Fortunately, captive insurance offers a measure of tax certainty not available with other forms of planning.

Keeping It Real: Why "Insurance" Is So Important

The foregoing discussion assumes that what your captive insurance company is providing you, in exchange for the premium payments from your business, is actual insurance. But what do we mean by the word "insurance"?

Fortunately for us, we don't have to ponder this question in too much detail; the US Supreme Court provides us with a set of requirements that lawyers, accountants, and the IRS use on a daily basis to help define "insurance." Basically, what we know as "insurance" consists of two economic components:

1. *Risk shifting*, whereby you cause liability for risk to be transferred from you to someone else or from your business to your captive insurance company.
2. *Risk distribution*, in which the insurance company bundles the risk from your business with the risks of many other businesses to protect against any one claim causing a catastrophic loss for the insurance company.

Risk shifting is the easier of the two requirements, as you pretty much achieve risk shifting whenever you buy an insurance policy. After all, the insurance company is contractually obligated to pay you if you incur a loss covered under the policy. In other words, you have shifted the risk for that type of loss from yourself (or your business) to the insurance company. Captive insurance companies meet this requirement by issuing policies that cover risks of loss in your business.

Risk distribution (not to be confused with one of the new requirements added by The PATH Act, that being a risk diversification component designed to curtail perceived estate planning abuses) is the more complex of these two requirements, as it requires a statistical analysis of the risks and businesses insured by the insurance carrier. As you will learn in chapter 4, there are many ways that risk distribution can be achieved, including among related companies in a corporate group or among unrelated companies pooling their risks. Captive insurance companies typically satisfy this requirement by joining reinsurance pools with other captive insurance companies, in which each captive shares a part of its risk with the pool in exchange for taking on a proportional amount of the pool's risk.

If you have risk shifting and risk distribution, then you generally have insurance. However, we're not out of the woods just yet. The risks insured have to be relevant to your business. For example, if your employees don't travel into dangerous Third World countries, you cannot justify having your business pay for kidnap and ransom insurance on key employees. The risks insured in your business need to be actual risks for which insurance serves a valid, viable purpose.

In practice, captive owners should engage the services of a licensed and fully credentialed underwriter and actuary to analyze their business and make recommendations on the scope and amounts of coverage to be insured by the captive. As long as you keep in mind that (1) insurance requires risk distribution and risk shifting through the captive, and (2) the insurance coverage needs to be reasonable in relation to the risks of your business, the premiums paid by your company into your captive may be tax deductible.

Overview of the Captive Insurance Industry

Ever since Fred Reiss moved his captive insurance business to Bermuda in 1962, the captive insurance industry has witnessed explosive growth, both overseas and in the United States. Two of the biggest players in the captive insurance industry are reinsurance firms: Aon Corporation, a Chicago-headquartered firm with five hundred offices in more than 120 countries and staffed by close to seventy-two thousand employees, and Marsh & McLennan Companies, a New York-headquartered firm with offices in more than 130 countries and staffed by sixty thousand employees. As you may recall from the preceding discussion, a critical component of captive insurance design is reinsurance. Therefore, it is only natural that reinsurance firms have a good handle on captive insurance.

Why do people go offshore for captive insurance?

Here is an important principle I use in my business every day and which I hope helps you as you learn about captive insurance: *never go offshore for things that you can do onshore; only go offshore for those things that are not available onshore.* That said, most of my clients form their captive insurance companies offshore. Why is that? Well, ultimately the choice will come down to comfort, fit, and feel. While the United States has a number of wonderful jurisdictions, many of which are progressive, pro-business, and active in the captive community, going offshore continues to be the preferred choice based on decades of established regulatory experience and guidance in the field.

When Reiss moved his captive management company to Bermuda in 1962, he gave birth to an offshore industry built around supporting captive insurance companies. Country after country in the Caribbean enacted laws designed to foster the growth of captive insurance companies in their jurisdictions.

Prior to captive insurance, many of these offshore jurisdictions had little domestic industry aside from modest farming, fishing, and—of course—sizeable tourism. However, as captive insurance began to take hold, many Caribbean islands witnessed an explosion in demand for highly skilled workers, and these workers brought home bigger paychecks, fostering even greater economic development. These days, many principle jurisdictions in the Caribbean owe a substantial part of their gross domestic product to the captive insurance industry.

If a state like Vermont could enact a captive insurance law that was simpler, better, and more cost effective than the captive insurance laws in some Caribbean countries, I would expect to see a seismic shift of business to Vermont. However, to stay competitive, many Caribbean jurisdictions have kept a close eye on states like Vermont, Delaware, and Tennessee to ensure that their laws remain competitive and that they offer a more business-friendly environment than that available domestically.

Leading Countries and States for Captives

There are approximately forty foreign domiciles where you may choose to license your captive. The following countries are well known for offering competent captive insurance laws and a favorable climate for setting up and running a captive insurance company: Anguilla, Bahamas, Bermuda, British Columbia, Cayman Islands, Nevis, and St. Lucia.

Likewise, there are approximately forty US states that offer captive insurance licensure. Here are a few of the jurisdictions that are well known and offer favorable captive insurance company legislation: District of Columbia, Georgia, Kentucky, New York, Nevada, South Carolina, Tennessee, Utah, and Vermont.

There is no magic bullet. *There is no one country or state that is "better" than any other in providing captive insurance legislation. The difference is in the cost and hassle incurred in setting up and maintaining your captive insurance company.* I prefer that my clients work with those jurisdictions that are less expensive and easier to work with. In my experience, those jurisdictions are universally offshore, with the Bahamas being one of my favorites.

How to Implement a Captive Insurance Plan

You may be thinking that setting up and running a captive insurance company requires you to hire lots of experts, attorneys, and accountants. Furthermore, you may not feel entirely confident that you know what an actuary is, much less know of one.

Fortunately, there are many service providers in the captive insurance industry. The industry has significantly matured over the past sixty years such that many service providers offer "turnkey" service packages in which the most critical functions of your captive insurance company are handled for you. The scope of services provided and the fees these service providers charge for doing the work vary quite significantly. Therefore, you need to shop around or work with an experienced advisor. It is critical that you focus on both (1) the appropriate establishment of your captive and (2) ongoing operations. My law firm focuses on the implementation and coordination of the captive. We then work with a captive manager once the captive insurance company is licensed.

The industry, however, is dominated by "one-stop shops," and there is an inherent danger in engaging such a service. We refer to this as the pass-the-phone technique, one in which a prospective captive insurance company owner calls a manager, tells them the deduction they would like, and subsequently has the phone handed off by the manager to their in-house actuary to price just enough coverage to cover the requested deduction. The danger is obvious and leaves one questioning where the impartial third-party analysis is. That said, at a minimum, most service providers will offer the following services as part of a turnkey package:

- analyzing your business and its insurance needs;

- establishing and licensing your captive insurance company; and
- arranging reinsurance for your captive.

Most service providers will offer additional services at an added cost. In my opinion, the more services offered for a set fee, the better off you are. Sometimes business owners discover that their chosen service provider does not provide a critical service—such as tax return preparation, for example, in which case they have to scramble to find a competent CPA to help them file returns for the captive. Therefore, a good captive insurance service provider will leave as little to chance as possible, providing as complete a set of services as possible at a set rate that you are happy with.

Also, it is typical that you sign a long-term contract with the service provider to maintain your captive for you. Of course, as a business owner, you know that there is a certain amount of due diligence that you need to conduct before you enter into any arrangement with a service provider. This is where the services of an experienced professional advisor are invaluable.

Chapter 3 contains a complete discussion of the steps in forming a captive insurance company, as well as in maintaining the company for as little or as long a time as you desire. The important point here is that *you will want to team up with an experienced captive insurance advisor and an experienced service provider.*

What You Need to Know about Cell Captives

In the course of researching captive insurance and talking to service professionals, you may hear terms such as "fronting companies," "cell captives," "rent-a-captives," "risk retention groups," and other industry jargon. I will refrain from using these terms beyond simply defining them for you. I do, however, want to familiarize you with one important type of entity that you may run across in captive insurance planning, particularly because it can save you time and money: the cell captive.

Many years ago, Delaware enacted an amendment to its limited liability company law permitting the formation of "series LLCs." This special law permits a Delaware LLC to operate as if it legally consists of two or more completely separate businesses, each with its own assets and liabilities distinct from the other. For example, let's say that I form XYZ LLC as a series LLC in Delaware, intending that Series A will hold undeveloped real estate and that Series B will operate a nursing home. Let us further assume that the Series B business (the nursing home) suffers a catastrophic liability when a patient dies in its care and the nursing home is found liable. The judgment creditor may pursue the assets of the Series B (nursing home) business, but—under Delaware law—the creditor is barred from going after the assets of Series A (the undeveloped land), even though both businesses are held in the name of XYZ LLC.

Imagine what could happen if that same concept, the Delaware series LLC, were applied to captive insurance? Well, many jurisdictions now offer the series LLC concept for insurance companies. Each jurisdiction tends to have its own name to describe this concept, but the most common name for such an entity is a "cell company" or "segregated accounts company." With a cell company, the assets and liabilities of one insurance company cell are legally distinct from the assets and liabilities of another cell within the same insurance company.

The cell company is somewhat like a bank account. You and your neighbor may both keep your money at the same bank, but your bank account is legally distinct from your neighbor's account at the same bank. The bank has no right to take the money from your account and put it in your neighbor's account (unless, of course, you give your neighbor a check or otherwise instruct the bank to pay your neighbor).

Cell captives are popular in the captive insurance industry because they are simple, cost-efficient structures and because they lend themselves well to external management. Most captive owners rely on the expertise of an experienced captive insurance company manager to run their captives for them. For this purpose, many service providers form their own insurance company licensed to operate any number of cells; in turn, each client of the service provider owns his or her own cell, separate and apart from all of the service provider's other clients. The "host" insurance company manages each of the cells for its clients.

How Long Does It Take to Establish a Captive?

You can expect the typical captive formation to take between three and four months. The process begins with two critical components, consisting of (1) underwriting, in which the risks of your business are identified (known as the "qualitative" process), and (2) an actuarial assessment of the business, in which the identified insurable risk is measured and priced (known as the "quantitative" process). Once an insurance program is outlined and, more importantly, it is determined that a captive makes both qualitative and quantitative sense, the lawyers and the service providers will work to establish the captive insurance company. Once formed, your captive insurance company should be operated by an experienced captive insurance manager and overseen by an attorney.

At some point in the formation process, the lawyers will ascertain the client's planning goals in relation to risk management, asset protection, and out-of-pocket savings. Most likely, ownership of the captive insurance company will be titled in the name of the business owner or the business itself. This helps to ensure that ownership of the captive does not fall into the hands of an uninvited party or fall afoul of any legalities (e.g., violate The PATH Act).

What Happens after the Captive Is Formed?

One of the first things your newly formed captive insurance company will embark upon is writing insurance coverage for your business. In return, your business will pay a premium to the captive insurance company. If the captive insurance company is properly designed, the business should be able to claim the premium paid as an expense deductible against its taxable income, saving you on taxes.

The premium paid into your captive will go into a bank account titled in the name of your captive. From there, the service provider managing your captive will typically deduct service fees and apply a portion of your premium to reinsurance. The remaining amount must be cautiously invested in order to ensure that your captive is financially capable of paying any claims submitted while the insurance coverage is in place.

Most jurisdictions require the captive insurance company managers to submit an investment plan for approval by the insurance regulators. Your service provider will have designed this for you and will have obtained approval for a plan that typically requires the captive to maintain a conservatively diversified portfolio of credible investments. In most cases, you are able to appoint your own professional investment advisor to supervise these investments and ensure that the investments within your captive are consistent with your personal planning goals. Therefore, if you want your trusted broker at Morgan Stanley to manage the portfolio, most service providers will accommodate this request.

For the first year that your new insurance company is in place, the premiums paid to the captive must be conservatively managed. You will not be permitted to invest the money in a number of spins at the roulette wheel. At the end of the first year and in each subsequent year in which coverage is in place, the assets will continue to be managed in a conservative manner. However, after the term of coverage has passed and if no claims have been filed, the money left over inside your captive will shift to "surplus." These funds can be more aggressively invested and offer greater flexibility (if that is what you want).

As you may gather from the foregoing discussion, implementing a captive insurance plan involves a number of steps and many moving parts. However, as I mentioned earlier in this chapter, *captive insurance is a simple concept.* This is true both in theory and in execution. An experienced lawyer will guide you through each step of the process. Your obligations will largely be limited to (1) providing the information requested by the lawyers and service providers and (2) paying their fees. Otherwise, the majority of the heavy lifting is handled for you by various service providers.

Chapter Two

HOW TO MAXIMIZE THE FULL POTENTIAL OF A CAPTIVE INSURANCE COMPANY?

The Income Tax Benefits of Captive Insurance

Captive insurance originated as a strategy to save on the costs of insurance. By having your business purchase insurance from your own captive, you can capture the profits from insurance for yourself rather than allowing those profits to benefit an unrelated insurance company.

When a business pays premiums to an insurance company for coverage on business-related risks, the business is normally entitled to claim an expense deductible against its taxable income. In many businesses, the tax deduction generated by insurance expenses may be modest. However, any high-risk business owner will tell you that the large premiums paid on liability insurance represent significant deductions for tax purposes.

Normally, a tax deduction is nothing to get excited about. After all, a legitimate expense represents money that has been paid to someone else in the course of your business. Claiming the tax deduction is only necessary to arrive at an accurate calculation of your business taxable income.

Captive insurance, however, adds a new dimension to business tax planning. When the premium expense is deducted from your business taxable income, you of course reduce your tax bill with Uncle Sam. However, that premium still remains as money inside your captive. Moreover, if your captive experiences little or no claims, then the remaining money inside your captive is pure profit that can be invested or paid out to you in the future. Imagine claiming a tax deduction on money that you keep!

This income tax benefit takes on added dimension when you consider that by being able to keep the money you pay for insurance, you might be able to buy more insurance than you might normally consider for your business. Have you ever had an insurance agent offer you additional coverage for your business that you turned down, most likely because you could not afford it? Or perhaps you felt that the coverage was more than you needed—a luxury that you would only consider if money grew on trees.

Captive insurance enables you to profit from having your business purchase insurance from your captive. If you manage your business liabilities such that your captive does not have any claims at the end of the policy year, the premiums paid in represent profits of the captive. You own the captive, so you own those profits.

You may be thinking to yourself, "How far can this go? Can I pay out all of my company's profits in the form of insurance premiums to my captive?" Obviously, there is a limit to how far you can take this concept. First, the actuaries examining your business will have their own idea of how much insurance is justified by your business activities and liabilities. If your business cannot justify incurring the added insurance expense, then the IRS will likely disallow any excessive deduction for insurance premiums paid, recharacterizing the payments as disguised dividends or something else that does not give rise to a deduction.

Of course, I just breezed through a series of tax concepts. There are some important details that you will want to familiarize yourself with. I will walk you through these important points in the following paragraphs. However, I want you to bear in mind these two principles of income tax planning with captive insurance:

1. Properly structured, your business can deduct from its taxable income the premiums paid to your captive insurance company.

2. Within reason, your business can purchase additional coverage from your captive insurance company, even if you historically have not purchased this coverage from an unrelated insurance company. Most business owners buy only what they think they need, not what they actually do need.

IRC § 831: The $2.2 Million Exemption for Small Captives

In the first chapter, I introduced to you an important tax rule that is seldom discussed but widely available. Under IRC § 831, the first $2.2 million[2] of premiums received by an electing small captive insurance company is exempt from federal income tax. Consider this: even though you get to *deduct* the premium paid to your captive from your business taxable income, the captive itself does not pay any tax on the premium.

2 | Effective January 1, 2017, changes to The PATH Act, made in December 2015, increase the tax exemption for premiums paid from $1.2 to $2.2 million annually (adjusted for inflation).

How can this be? Well, I am sure you have heard of special interest groups. Politicians always blame special interest groups for whatever ails the American political system. Washington gridlock? Blame it on special interest groups. Congress and the president unable to reach a budget deal? That same old boogeyman, the special interest group, must be to blame!

I do not want to editorialize here, but the truth of the matter is that we are all special interest groups. Many readers are members of the American Association of Retired Persons; that's a special interest group looking out for seniors on Capitol Hill. As a lawyer, I belong to a special interest group—the American Bar Association—seeking to ensure that laws favorable to the legal profession are passed.

One of the most powerful special interest groups in Washington is the insurance industry. From the moment that the US government passed an income tax law, the insurance lobby has fought to ensure that Congress treats insurance companies and insurance-based financial products favorably.

Among the many gifts the insurance industry has obtained from Congress is IRC § 831. Under this provision, a "small" insurance company can file a special election with the IRS that entitles the company to exempt the first $2.2 million of premiums collected *every year.* I am paraphrasing this rule, but here is how it works. First, IRC § 831(a) provides an alternative tax system by which an insurance company can elect to pay tax on its investment income without paying any taxes on its premium income. Next, IRC § 831(b) tells us which insurance companies get to make this election. Here is the text of the actual statute:

> (b) This subsection shall apply to every insurance company other than life (including interinsurers and reciprocal underwriters) if—

(i) the net written premiums (or, if greater, direct written premiums) for the taxable year do not exceed $2,200,000, and

(ii) such company elects the application of this subsection for such taxable year.

The election under clause (ii) shall apply to the taxable year for which made and for all subsequent taxable years for which the requirements of clause (i) are met.[3]

To be accurate, IRC § 831(a) provides that an insurance company meeting the requirements of IRC § 831(b) is not subject to tax on *any* of its premium income. However, the first requirement of IRC § 831(b) is that the insurance company not receive premiums in excess of $2.2 million in any given year. Therefore, IRC § 831 essentially provides a tax exemption of up to $2.2 million in premiums each year.

Can you imagine lobbying Congress for a special rule that lets you exempt $2.2 million every year from your medical business or manufacturing company? Congress apparently determined that small insurance companies could use a little help from Uncle Sam. As long as you can justify the insurance expenses in your business, you can use a captive to take advantage of up to $2.2 million annually.

Quantifying the Income Tax Benefit

What is the value of this $2.2 million exemption for captive insurance companies? The best way to answer this question is to ask your accountant what your effective tax rate is on your business

3 | IRC § 831(b).

income. Thirty percent? Forty percent? With the ever-changing laws on matters such as health care, taxes on wages and self-employment income will be much higher—45 percent? What happens when you factor in state income taxes as well? Are you over 50 percent? Many business owners in high-tax states incur a greater than 50 percent effective tax rate.

Let us just say for discussion's sake that the effective rate of tax on your business income, both federal and state combined, is 40 percent. Forty percent of $2.2 million is $880,000.

Think about this: depending on your business and individual circumstances, you might conceivably pocket *nearly a million dollars in tax savings every year.*

To be fair, not every business can deduct $2.2 million in insurance premiums. If your business grossed $3 million per year, it would be difficult to justify more than roughly $250,000 in premiums each year. The actual amount that you can deduct is based on an actuarial assessment of your business including its revenue and expenses, its existing insurance coverage, and the liabilities normally associated with it. Most captive insurance service providers will engage the services of a qualified actuary, who assesses all of these factors and produces a set of recommendations. These recommendations form the foundation by which your captive insures your business and your business pays premiums to the captive.

IRS and Court Rulings on Captive Insurance

Early on in the history of captive insurance, the IRS argued that captive insurance was nothing but self-insurance, and the IRS had long held the view that self-insurance could not give rise to a tax deduction. The IRS used an "economic family" argument to contend that captive insurance is a mere bookkeeping transaction in which money from one business winds up in a related business.[4] Because there was no risk shifting outside of the economic family of related businesses, the IRS argued that the arrangement was not real insurance.

No court ever accepted the IRS "economic family" argument. Instead, several court decisions dealt a stinging rebuke to the IRS, supporting captive insurance arrangements in a number of instances.[5] The IRS finally conceded the point in Revenue Ruling 2001-31, acknowledging that premiums paid to a captive insurance company can be deducted when properly structured.

You may recall from chapter 1 that the Supreme Court defines insurance as having two components: (1) risk shifting and (2) risk distribution. Without both of these elements you don't have insurance, and the money you pay to your captive cannot be considered a deductible premium payment.

Over the years, the IRS has refined its views regarding captive insurance by focusing particularly on the concept of risk distribution. In Revenue Ruling 2002-89, the IRS considered the classic case of a parent company purchasing insurance from its subsidiary captive insurance company. In determining whether the parent was allowed a tax deduction for the premiums paid to the subsidiary captive, the IRS looked to the amount of risks insured by the subsidiary captive with unrelated parties. In a sense, the IRS was still applying its "economic family" doctrine, albeit more narrowly. In Situation 1, the subsidiary received 90 percent of its premiums and assumed 90 percent of its risks, in relation to the liabilities of its parent company. In Situation 2, the same subsidiary received less than 50 percent of its premiums and assumed less than 50 percent of its total risks, in

---

4 | See Rev. Rul. 77-316.

5 | See, e.g., Humana, Inc. v. Commissioner, 881 F.2d 247 (6th Cir. 1989); Clougherty Packing Co. v. Commissioner, 811 F.2d 1297 (9th Cir. 1987); Kidde Industries, Inc. v. United States, 40 Fed. Cl. 42 (1997).

respect of its parent company. The IRS determined that in Situation 1, where the premiums and risks of the parent comprised substantially all of the subsidiary's insurance activities, there was insufficient risk distribution. In Situation 2, however, where the premiums and risks of unrelated parties comprised more than 50 percent of the subsidiary captive's business, the IRS deemed there to be sufficient risk distribution, and accordingly, the parent was permitted to deduct its insurance premiums paid to its subsidiary captive insurance company.

Revenue Ruling 2002-90 dealt with another form of risk distribution—risks of multiple subsidiaries of a common parent holding company assumed by a captive insurance company. The parent company and its twelve subsidiaries were engaged in providing professional services in a number of states; each subsidiary confined its activities to a particular state. The twelve subsidiaries each paid premiums into a captive insurance company owned by the parent holding company; the captive insurance company carried no more than 15 percent of its risks on any one particular subsidiary within the group. The IRS cited the Sixth Circuit's ruling in *Humana Inc. v. Commissioner*[6] for the proposition that risk distribution may be achieved by pooling the risks of multiple subsidiaries of the same parent holding company. The ruling states, "Risk distribution necessarily entails a pooling of premiums, so that a potential insured is not in significant part paying for its own risks."

Therefore, there are two ways to achieve risk distribution under current tax law with a captive insurance company:

1. Assume more than 50 percent risks of unrelated companies; or

6 881 F.2d 247, 257 (6th Cir. 1989).

2. Assume multiple risks from related companies so that no one related company comprises more than 15 percent of the pooled risks of the captive.

How far can you go with these percentages? In other words, just how much unrelated risk must your captive insurance company assume in order to be acceptable in the eyes of the law? In *The Harper Group v. Commissioner*, a captive insurance company only retained 29 percent unrelated party risks within its pool of insurance policies. Nevertheless, the Ninth Circuit Court of Appeals upheld the arrangement as having sufficient risk distribution, citing the relatively large number of unrelated parties who had purchased insurance from the captive. While this case was successfully argued, and as will be discussed further in chapter 5, I would advise you to follow the guidelines published by the IRS in which at least 50 percent of unrelated party risk should be retained within your captive insurance company.

Achieving Risk Distribution within Your Own Captive Insurance Company: Reinsurance Pools

At this point, you might be asking how it is possible that you can achieve risk distribution within your own captive insurance company. From what you just read, you understand that either (1) you need to have a lot of subsidiary companies purchasing insurance from your captive or (2) your captive needs to insure the risks of unrelated parties. Assuming your business does not have twelve subsidiaries operating all across the United States, how can you possibly insure unrelated party risks with your captive?

Fortunately, most captive insurance service providers work with reinsurance pools. This helps your captive insure the unrelated risks that satisfy the risk distribution requirement. Because this is a turnkey solution offered by many service providers, you often do not even have to think about this requirement; it is simply done for you.

In order to understand how we solve the risk distribution problem for your captive, you need to understand a little bit about reinsurance pools. Normally when I mention the word "pool," my clients tend to think of a swimming pool: a physical structure that holds things. Reinsurance pools are different; there is no physical structure. Many times there is not even an office or phone number that represents the reinsurance pool.

So then, what is a "reinsurance pool"? In its simplest form, a reinsurance pool is nothing more than an agreement among any number of captive insurance companies to pool their risks together. The "pooling" is bilateral: each captive transfers a certain amount of its risks *into* the pool, and each captive assumes an identical amount of risks *from* the pool.

Allow me to explain this to you with a simple example:

> After consulting with your lawyer, you decide to form Captive A, and your business purchases insurance from Captive A, paying $100 in premium to Captive A. Unbeknownst to you, your neighbor also uses the same lawyer to form Captive B, and he purchases insurance for his business from Captive B, funding Captive B with $100 in premium.
>
> During a round of golf one day, you and your neighbor learn that each of you has been using the same lawyer to implement a captive insurance plan. You both are looking to achieve risk distribution within your own captives. Your lawyer suggests a solution: your two captives pool their

> risks. Specifically, the lawyer recommends that Captive A pay $50 to Captive B in order to have Captive B reinsure 50 percent of the risks of Captive A. At the same time, the lawyer proposes that Captive B pay $50 to Captive A in order to have Captive A reinsure 50 percent of the risks of Captive B.
>
> You and your neighbor agree that this is a terrific idea, particularly because the two of you know each other well and trust each other to manage your risks effectively. The two of you therefore cause your captives to enter into a reinsurance pooling agreement formalizing this arrangement.
>
> As a result of these transactions, Captive A now has $50 net premium from insuring the risks of your business and $50 net premium from the reinsurance pool in respect of the risks of Captive B.

As you may be able to tell from this example, a reinsurance pooling arrangement is a straightforward agreement among several captives to simply reinsure each other's risks. Each captive transfers some of its risk *into* the pool in exchange for assuming a certain amount of the total risk *from* the pool. While some practitioners believe in constructive receipt, I would urge you to only engage in a risk-pooling arrangement whereby there is actual transfer of risk. Reliance on the appearance is far less certain than the actual physical transfer of funds. It is also far easier to hold one accountable when physical transfer has occurred. Even though there is an offsetting flow of dollars in and out of the reinsurance pool, money should absolutely change hands. (Oftentimes, the transferring of funds from one captive insurance company to another captive insurance company is facilitated by a captive insurance manager responsible for administering the reinsurance pool.) My management firm (Hamilton Captive Management, LLC) not only administers the pool but also requires the actual transfer of funds by the individual captive owners and pool participants. Accurate books and records reflecting the transaction should always be kept as well.

Does a Reinsurance Pool Run the Risk That My Captive Will Have to Pay a Substantial Claim?

As I mentioned in chapter 1, it is important that the activities conducted by your captive insurance company constitute real insurance. I made a simple observation in chapter 1, explaining that a business with no risk of having its employees kidnapped and held for ransom by Somali pirates would not purchase insurance to cover such a risk. The corollary to this is that if the insurance coverage is real, then the insurance policy should pay out when you have a legitimate claim.

Reinsurance pools introduce the risk that your captive insurance company might have to contribute toward paying a claim incurred by another captive member of the reinsurance pool. In other words, your money could end up going to pay for someone else's claim. However, without this risk of loss, you would not have insurance and, in turn, would not be entitled to claim a deduction on premiums paid by your business to your captive insurance company.

Just because you need to participate in a reinsurance pool does not mean you need to take on reckless liabilities. Many operators of reinsurance pools have minimum requirements that must be met in order for your captive insurance company to participate. They will want to review your captive's operating history as well as the insurance claims history of your business. If you have a history of high insurance claims within your company, you can expect many reinsurance pools to be reluctant to bring your captive in as a member. On the other hand, most businesses have a low claims history. In fact, it is because of this low claims history that many business owners stand to profit from captive insurance.

Accelerating the Tax Savings: The Dividends-Received Deduction

When you receive dividends every year in your stock portfolio, you are subject to ordinary income tax on those dividends. At the time I am writing this book, the federal income tax rate is between 15 and 39.6 percent, depending on your tax bracket. This does not include state income tax, which in some high-tax states can easily add another 10 to 15 percent of tax on top of the federal tax rate. Therefore, depending on the state where you reside, you may pay anywhere from 15 percent to over 50 percent on dividend income.

Insurance companies themselves also pay taxes on their earnings. This means that insurance companies calculate their income and pay taxes like any other taxpayer. At the end of the taxable year, the insurance company has net after-tax profits. Those profits are then distributed to the insurance company's shareholders, where the shareholders incur ordinary income tax on their dividends.

You should notice by now that income generated by a corporation is, more or less, taxed twice—once when the corporation earns its profits and pays taxes on those earnings and a second time when the corporation pays out dividends and its shareholders have to pay ordinary income tax on those dividends. What happens when a corporation owns stock in another corporation (e.g., a subsidiary corporation)? As you can imagine, there is yet another layer of tax, as the subsidiary corporation pays taxes on its earnings as well.

To mitigate the effect of layer upon layer of corporation and shareholder income taxes, US income tax law provides a "dividends-received deduction" to corporations. Under this rule, a corporation excludes from its taxable earnings a portion of its income from dividends on stock investments. The amount of this deduction varies based on a number of factors. However, the dividends-received deduction adds up to substantial savings.

A captive insurance company can deduct 70 percent of the dividends that it receives from its stock portfolio investments.[7] This is the same as if you or I could simply exclude 70 percent of our income from our tax return! Let me walk you through a simple example:

> Alan owns Galaxy Insurance, a Bahamas-based captive insurance company that insures the risks in Alan's Auto Parts manufacturing business. After several years of insurance activity Galaxy Insurance holds a large portfolio of investment securities, including shares of stock in General Electric.
>
> Alan's investment manager, Craig, originally recommended stock in GE for Alan's captive. Craig is so confident in GE that he owns some GE stock himself. Alan does not have to wait long for his investment to pay off. One day, Craig calls up Alan to tell him that General Electric had a great year and had declared a very handsome dividend to its shareholders.
>
> Early the next year, Alan and Craig are out playing a round of golf when they get around to discussing taxes. Craig praises General Electric for having paid a very large

7 | IRC § 243(a)(1).

> dividend the previous year, but he laments his tax bill: 50 percent of his dividend went to pay federal and state income taxes.
>
> Alan smiles as he lines up his tee shot, explaining to Craig that his captive insurance company enjoys a dividends-received deduction. In fact, Alan's accountant has recently advised Alan that Galaxy's tax bill for the General Electric dividend is only 4.2 percent, or *less than one tenth of Craig's tax bill.*

How is this possible? Captive insurance companies are subject to corporate tax rates, which generally run 15 percent for the lowest income tax bracket. Because your captive excludes up to $2.2 million in premium income, your captive normally *only* incurs a corporate income tax liability on its investment income. However, under IRC Section 243, your captive is permitted to deduct 70 percent of its dividend income from regular stock investments. This means that your captive ends up paying regular taxes only on a limited selection of income items: interest and capital gains, among other items. Otherwise, your captive's premium income incurs *no tax*, and dividend income enjoys a 70 percent exemption from tax.

There are a number of different tax brackets by which you calculate corporate income tax for your captive. The first $50,000 of investment income is subject to a 15 percent rate of federal income tax. From $50,000 to $75,000, the tax rate is 25 percent.

For investment income in excess of $75,000, the tax rate for your captive averages around 35 percent. If your captive holds shares of stock as part of its investment portfolio, any dividends on the stock are eligible for a 70 percent deduction against the captive's taxable investment income. This means that your captive pays a federal income tax of between 4.2 and 10.2 percent on dividends, depending on your captive's applicable corporate tax bracket.

The impact of the dividends-received deduction means that your captive insurance company incurs a lower tax rate on dividends than you do on your personal return. If you pay less in taxes year over year, you are able to save more—and invest more—in your investment portfolio. *Ideally, your captive insurance company should be able to accumulate wealth more tax efficiently than you can yourself.* Granted, you will eventually incur an additional tax liability when you finally liquidate your captive, but we discuss ways to mitigate the tax impact of that in the next chapter.

Chapter Three

PUTTING THE CAPTIVE INSURANCE COMPANY TO WORK FOR YOU

How to Set Up a Captive and Start Insuring Your Business

Earlier in this book, I assured you that establishing your own captive and finding the appropriate captive management firm to handle the day-to-day operations, reinsurance, annual audit, tax matters, and so on for your own captive insurance company is not as complicated as it sounds. Of course, you may not be an insurance expert and you may not be prepared for the responsibilities of establishing and identifying the appropriate manager for your own captive. However, there are many capable service providers who are prepared to assist you with the implementation of your captive. Properly arranged, you should only need to concentrate on what you do best: running your business. You can leave the captive insurance company to the professionals to handle for you.

Over the next pages, I will walk you through a step-by-step outline that guides you through the process of forming your own captive insurance company and understanding the responsibilities that are required of the captive manager. Every case is different, but I have established many captive insurance companies over my career and can point out some common features that are likely to arise with your own captive.

Step 1: Determining Whether You and Your Business Benefit from Captive Insurance

Everyone could stand to reduce the amount of money spent on insurance while improving their overall risk management capabilities, but not everyone can use captive insurance in their business. A manufacturing company that produces consumer goods likely has a need for a lot of insurance: product liability, workers' compensation, and theft of intellectual property are some of the risks an actuary might find with such a business. On the other hand, if your business is passive and does not have employees, you may not have such a pronounced need for insurance.

The competent captive insurance plan begins with a thorough analysis of your business and its insurance needs. The focus is on both the existing coverage that you carry with commercial insurance companies and the risks that you are likely self-insuring, either because you cannot justify the cost of the additional coverage or you are not aware that such coverage is available.

The Qualifying Study

For this purpose, I always recommend retaining a lawyer who is well versed in captive insurance to assist you in bringing in a team of insurance professionals to examine your business. More to the point, an independent fully credentialed underwriter and an independent fully credentialed third-party actuary should be retained. The underwriter's primary objective is to evaluate the risk of your business and identify areas that should be insured. They will look at your existing insurance policies to see what is covered and what is excluded. They will examine your financial statements and tax returns to see how your company is performing and what its prospects are for growth. They will interview key personnel and study the internal processes of your business to see where liability can arise from your business activities. Ultimately, the underwriter will typically identify a number of risks—some of which you are already covering, and some of which you are not and should. They will make their recommendations to the actuary.

The actuary's primary objective is to appropriately price the risk that will be considered for your captive insurance company to provide coverage for your underlying business. At the end of this process, the actuary, working in concert with the underwriter, will produce a comprehensive report illustrating what areas of risk are uninsured or underinsured. They will also assess your current coverage to determine whether it is in your best interest to keep the coverage in place or to shift some of that coverage to your captive. The report will basically inform you as to what kinds of coverage can be underwritten by your own captive insurance company and how much in premiums you can pay for such coverage from your business. This actuarial analysis should be done on an annual basis, as your business changes from year to year and the coverages and corresponding premiums that were appropriate in one year may not be applicable in the next.

The Business Plan

In Step 2, I will discuss the difference between a "standalone" captive and a "cell" captive. It is important to note here, however, that a standalone captive often requires that a business plan be prepared. Usually the insurance regulator will ask to review the business plan before agreeing to issue an insurance license to a standalone captive.

Even if a business plan is not required, you should consider obtaining one. Again, the underwriter's report only assesses the risks of your business and the potential lines of insurance coverage that might be provided by your captive. The actuary's report provides the pricing of each policy and the pricing support. A feasibility report, by comparison, examines the process by which your captive approves or denies claims, the potential for catastrophic claims, and the financial ability of your captive to withstand such claims. *Whereas the purpose behind the underwriter's report is to determine the insurance needs of your business, the primary objective of a qualifying study is to determine whether a captive insurance company is right for you and your business.*

Most captive insurance service providers will offer to prepare these reports in consultation with you and your advisors in a matter of weeks, although a thorough examination of a large or complicated business may require a few months to complete. A proper examination will determine the size and scope of risks incurred in your business. Projecting these risks and potential claims over a long period of time (typically, at least ten years), the reports will also assist in determining the amount of capital that should be contributed to your captive insurance company at inception. (And with approximately eighty jurisdictions worldwide to choose from, capitalization is also a regulatory matter that needs to be taken into account.) Ultimately the underwriter's report, actuarial analysis, and initial due diligence will result in what is commonly referred to as a risk assessment report or feasibility report. This report should contain a complete perspective on all the operations of your captive, including proposed premium rates, capitalization, profits and losses, and even recommendations on the jurisdiction in which your captive should be established.

Making the Decision to Proceed with a Captive Insurance Plan

You will want to review the underwriter's recommendations, actuarial analysis, and feasibility report closely with your advisors. At this point, your attorney, CPA, and oftentimes senior executives or trusted advisors should be able to determine whether the recommendations contained in these reports are such that you would like to proceed with a captive insurance company. Your team will be able to reflect on the potential risks associated with your business and the potential for captive insurance to close any gaps in coverage.

Many times, clients are disappointed to learn that they cannot purchase as much insurance from their captive as they would like. Perhaps you are hoping to shift $1 million of business income into a captive through premium payments, but your actuary calculates a premium of only $500,000 worth of insurance coverage. Only if both the qualitative evaluation and quantitative analysis make sense should you proceed with the next step: forming your own captive insurance company.

Step 2: Forming the Captive Insurance Company

Cell Captive versus Standalone Captive

You may recall from chapter 1 that there is a form of captive insurance company referred to as a "cell" captive. One of the threshold issues that you and your advisors will first address in forming a captive is whether to form a "cell" or a "standalone" captive. This greatly influences just how long the licensing process will take, as well as the length and scope of other necessary formation tasks.

To refresh your memory, a cell captive is an offshoot of an existing insurance company that has been formed to host any number of underlying "cells." Each cell has its own assets and liabilities and is legally distinct from each other cell within the same insurance company.

As we saw in chapter 1, a cell is similar to a bank account in some ways. Even though you and your neighbor may keep your money at the same bank, you each have your own account and have no reason to commingle your funds. The same rule applies with cell captive insurance companies: while several cells may be administered by a common supervising insurance company, each cell is a distinct entity unto itself.

A standalone captive is simply a captive insurance company that is formed, licensed, and operated as a separate entity. A cell, on the other hand, is typically established by a larger insurance company that is licensed to form cells; the insurance company can form a new cell typically with much less paperwork, time, and effort. In practice, cells are much quicker to establish, less expensive to form, and much easier to run than standalone captives. However, neither the cell nor the standalone captive is superior as an insurance entity; each has its unique advantages, and the selection of one over the other usually depends on your specific needs.

If a cell captive is to be formed, the sponsoring insurance company will typically file paperwork with the insurance regulator permitting the sponsor to form the new cell. Depending on the jurisdiction, this can be done automatically and without the advance consent of the insurance regulator. That said, the decision on jurisdiction should not be taken lightly. As the saying goes, if it is worth doing, it is worth doing right. Jurisdictional selection is a very important component of the captive formation process. While the sponsoring insurance company may already have a license to issue insurance, the cell needs to obtain its own, separate license.

A standalone captive often requires much more lead time. During the formation process, a captive insurance manager will be selected and will assist in the preparation of a feasibility report and business plan to submit to the insurance regulator, requesting permission from the regulator to obtain a license to issue insurance. The regulator will examine the background of the prospective owners and managers of the captive. Typically, the regulator will require that a local registered agent, representative, and lawyer familiar to the regulator be appointed to serve alongside the insurance manager for the captive. Once the regulator reviews the feasibility report and approves the business plan, the company is formed and a bank account will ultimately be funded with the amount that is required for minimum capitalization of the insurance company. As mentioned previously, these capitalization requirements will vary from jurisdiction to jurisdiction, but they are not insubstantial and it is a consideration that shouldn't be taken lightly.

For the most part, forming the captive insurance company is not a difficult process. It often boils down to finding the right professional guidance. There's also a difference between the coordination and implementation of a captive and the ongoing operations. My law firm is typically engaged to assist in the formation of the captive. It is only after we have reviewed the risk assessment report or feasibility report and made a decision together to move forward that we engage a captive manager to provide the operational services. Most captive insurance service providers are familiar with the laws of a number of jurisdictions from which insurance company licenses can be obtained, and they will recommend the structure (cell versus standalone) and the jurisdiction based on the needs of the client.

At the end of the formation process, your captive insurance manager should be able to provide you with a complete binder of all the formation documents evidencing the establishment of your captive insurance company as well as your ownership of the captive. For a standalone captive, you should expect to see at a minimum the following documents in the formation binder:

- articles of incorporation or articles of association
- memorandum of association or bylaws
- minutes of the incorporator, directors, and shareholders
- a service agreement between the insurance manager and the new standalone captive
- a stock certificate issued in the name of you or your shareholding entity (whether it is your company or you individually)
- an operations manual with all of the pertinent details on your team (i.e., who your auditor, local counsel, actuary, etc. are).

- the policy register
- each insurance policy issued by your captive
- details on your reinsurance arrangement
- the claims filing process

For a cell captive, the documents may differ slightly, but a typical set includes the following additions to those previously mentioned:

- service agreement between the sponsoring insurance company and you establishing the cell captive (oftentimes known as a participation agreement)
- details on the corporate governance of your captive
- board policies and director's resolutions pertinent to your captive

Deciding on the Jurisdiction for Your Captive

In Step 1, I highlighted the importance of qualifying your business for a captive insurance company and the importance of professional guidance in doing so, from a well-versed attorney to an independent fully credentialed actuary. Again, this report helps you to determine whether captive insurance is viable and financially sound for your business. Many times, the feasibility report will be supplemented by a more comprehensive business plan, particularly if you are establishing a standalone captive. Insurance regulators in many jurisdictions ask to review a comprehensive business plan of the captive to ensure that its sponsors have adequately considered the costs and obligations of operating a captive.

Once a feasibility report or business plan is prepared, your advisor will likely recommend one or more jurisdictions that are best suited to the needs outlined. They will consider the licensing requirements and formation costs of a variety of jurisdictions, as well as the ongoing reporting and administrative obligations for your captive. While the licensing requirements and reporting obligations are similar among popular captive jurisdictions, the costs of compliance and the time it takes to form your captive vary widely from country to country and state to state. Therefore, you should carefully examine these factors with your advisor.

As discussed in chapter 1, most captive insurance companies are formed overseas, but an increasing number of captives are formed right here in the United States, with approximately forty states now permitting the formation of captive insurance companies. Yet, one of the biggest variables in selecting a foreign or domestic jurisdiction for your captive is cost, and most often it is far cheaper and more convenient to form your captive in one of the popular offshore insurance jurisdictions than to establish a captive domestically.

Even if you and your advisor determine that it would be substantially cheaper to form a captive overseas than in the United States, sometimes you are required to form the captive domestically. For example, "risk retention groups"—a form of captive insurance company governed by the Federal Liability Risk Retention Act of 1986—are required to be licensed and operated domestically. Sometimes other companies that contract with your business will not accept insurance or a bond issued by an overseas captive. Aside from these few limitations, however, it is my experience that offshore jurisdictions are cheaper and easier to work with and that most third parties engaged in commerce with your business are not concerned with where the captive insuring your business is organized. It is worth noting that offshore jurisdictions do not "raise the red flag." Rather, proper establishment, coverage selection, and appropriate pricing are the factors that often determine whether the "flag" is raised.

Step 3: Implementing the Insurance Coverage and Paying Premiums

In Step 1, you make a determination whether captive insurance is right for you and your business. Your decision to implement a captive insurance plan turns, in part, on the results of an underwriting evaluation and actuarial examination of your business and its insurance needs. Those results are used as the foundation for the insurance policies to be issued by your captive insurance company as well as the premiums that your business pays for that coverage.

Your advisor will likely work with a captive insurance service provider or insurance actuary to design a set of insurance policies that cover key risks in your business. Some of this coverage may be new to your business, plugging gaps in the existing coverage that you have. Risks that were previously uninsured (i.e., self-insured) will instead be insured by your captive. Other types of coverage may be intended to replace insurance that your business currently purchases from an unrelated insurance carrier.

Depending on the type of coverage extended, there may be more than one policy contract issued by your captive. For example, if you are a physician with your own medical practice, one type of policy may be a form of indemnity to cover claims from malpractice or other professional risks; this type of coverage is referred to as "business liability" insurance. A separate policy may be issued to insure the property in your business from flooding, fire, and theft; this type of coverage is often referred to as "business casualty" insurance.

In practice, there are literally hundreds of types of business liability and casualty policies written frequently by insurance carriers in the United States. It may not be as surprising to learn what types of insurance can be implemented with your captive as to learn the amount of insurance that can be purchased. Again, the actuarial analysis of your business should help you and your advisor determine a responsible amount of insurance coverage that is reasonable in relation to your business and its activities.

Business Liability Insurance

Business liability insurance is an important category of coverage commonly used by doctors and lawyers to protect themselves from malpractice claims. It is also used to protect many other types of businesses from claims. Such coverage may include employment practices liability, product liability, construction and design defects, excess professional liability, intellectual property liability (including copyright or patent infringement), cyber liability, business interruption, and so on. The list is endless.

The most common types of liability policies used in business are issued in the following formats of coverage:

1. *Indemnity:* An indemnity policy pays out to third parties for claims they may have against your business for tortious or wrongful acts.
2. *Litigation Expenses:* If your business is sued, this type of policy reimburses your business for legal fees incurred in defending against the lawsuit.
3. *Direct Policies:* A direct policy is a form of business liability insurance that pays out to claimants as well as reimbursing

your business for the expenses of litigation. Typically, litigation expense policies (listed in item 2) are a limited form of direct policy.

Unfortunately, in today's litigious environment, having insurance sometimes makes you a target for a lawsuit. After all, a plaintiff may be willing to pursue litigation in the hopes of cashing in on your insurance coverage. If your business does not submit a claim for reimbursement by the insurance carrier, the plaintiff may obtain a court order compelling your business to process the claim. By comparison, a policy that covers the litigation expenses incurred by your business is one that is exclusively within the control of your business; plaintiffs cannot claim the benefits of a litigation expense policy for your business.

Some businesses, such as construction firms, are required to post a bond securing their performance on a major contract. Oftentimes these types of performance bonds are very expensive, even if claims are low or nonexistent. Fortunately, your captive insurance company can issue these types of bonds alongside insurance. Your captive can also participate in reinsurance pools that reinsure bonds issued by other captive insurance companies. In addition to performance bonds, captives can issue bonds to secure the payment of customs duties or ERISA liabilities, fidelity bonds or surety bonds, and buyer-credit bonds.

Business Casualty Policies

Casualty policies are more popular with captives because of the greater control businesses enjoy over the claims that are submitted. With a business liability policy, your business may be required by law to submit a claim for the benefit of a third party who has sued your business. By comparison, with most business casualty policies, your business can determine whether it is in its own financial interest to submit a claim.

Consider, for example, personal insurance that you may have covering damage to your car. If you damage your own car, you are less likely to submit a claim to your insurance carrier because you do not want your insurance rates to increase. Likewise, with business casualty policies, the insured business can gauge whether a claim is sufficiently catastrophic to require reimbursement even at the expense of higher insurance rates in the future.

The range of "casualties" that a business may insure is practically limitless. In addition to normal coverage for business property damage, casualty insurance may cover the failure of equipment, computer systems, and machinery used in the business, or even unforeseen damages caused by weather, criminal activity, or government activities. Odds are your business has no current coverage for damage to its reputation; you are likely self-insuring the risk that a competitor may defame your business, sabotage your products, or steal valuable intellectual property and trade secrets from your business. Many businesses have no insurance covering them in case their business is interrupted, whether on account of weather, regulatory action, employee strikes, or terrorism. Fortunately, a captive insurance company can write coverage to insure your business against these types of casualties provided the basis for the specific policy can be established.

Invoicing for Premiums

Once the policies are drawn up and the amounts of coverage determined, the manager of your captive (typically, the captive insurance service provider) will cause your captive to generate an invoice to your business. You will then cause your business to pay this invoice, creating an expense that should be deductible for tax purposes if your captive insurance is properly designed.

You should note that many captive insurance companies do not issue policies, and invoice for premium payments, until late in the calendar year. There are two reasons for this. First, many companies do not know what their cash resources will be for captive insurance until late in the year. Second, paying a recurring expense, such as insurance premiums, late in the year typically entitles your business to deduct the full expense in the year of payment, even if the insurance coverage extends into the following calendar year. For these reasons, a large part of the captive insurance industry witnesses a lot of activity in the last quarter of each calendar year.

Premium Financing

What happens if your business has insufficient cash flow at the end of the year to pay for the next year's insurance premium with your captive? Many businesses rely on premium financing to help solve this problem. With premium financing, an outside financing company advances a loan to your business by paying the premium to your captive insurance company. Your business then makes loan payments to the premium finance company.

Some, but not many, captive insurance consultants and service providers can arrange premium financing for your business. In most cases, the financing will be arranged so that your business enjoys the protection, and associated tax benefits, that come from purchasing insurance coverage in the current year. At the same time, your business will have the time needed to make loan repayments from existing cash flow. If you fail to pay the loan back as scheduled, the insurance coverage may be terminated early, resulting in a partial loss of any tax deduction claimed on the original purchase.

Step 4: Procuring Tax-Compliant Reinsurance

The most challenging aspect of captive insurance is securing the tax-compliant reinsurance that you need to ensure the integrity of your planning. Captive insurance is of diminished use if you cannot legitimately claim a tax deduction in your business for the premiums paid to your captive insurance company or you cannot rely on the reinsurance provider to cover you should the need arise.

You may recall from chapter 1 that the federal courts have defined "insurance" to consist of two economic activities: (1) risk shifting and (2) risk distribution. Risk shifting is fairly easy to achieve; when your captive issues a policy insuring the risks of your business, you have shifted risk from your business to your captive. *Risk distribution, on the other hand, is much more esoteric. In my experience, this is where many captive insurance service providers fall short. Therefore, you want to be very careful in examining how your service provider meets the risk distribution requirement for your captive.*

In chapter 1, I introduced you to the concept of risk distribution—the activity by which the insurance company bundles the risk from your business with the risks of many other businesses to protect against the chance that any one claim would cause a catastrophic loss for the insurance company. Some insurance experts describe this as the "smoothing effect" that is gained when an insurance company acquires a lot of unrelated cases, so that the insurance company's financial well-being is not dependent on a small number of cases.

Chapter 2 discussed a pair of IRS Revenue Rulings concerning risk distribution. Revenue Ruling 2002-89 dealt with two situations involving a captive insurance company. In Situation 1, the captive insured only the risks of its parent company. In Situation 2, the captive received a majority of its premiums and risks from unrelated parties. The IRS concluded that there was insufficient risk distribution in Situation 1, whereas Situation 2 passed muster. Revenue Ruling 2002-90 clarified that risk distribution could even be achieved by insuring risks of multiple companies in the same ownership group; an example of a captive insuring twelve subsidiaries in equal proportion satisfied the IRS requirements for risk distribution.

The most common form of risk distribution that you will see with "small" captive insurance companies is reinsurance pooling. As discussed in chapter 2, a reinsurance pool involves several captives "pooling" their risks together, each assuming a share of the others' liability and each transferring a share of its risk to the overall pool. Reinsurance pooling occurs with large public insurance companies as well as small captives. However, for small captives, the advantage is that you do not need to issue a lot of insurance policies to several unrelated companies or carriers in order to achieve sufficient risk distribution. Rather, your captive can enter into one pooling agreement in which a number of unrelated carriers, reinsuring the risks of unrelated parties, also participate.

Some captive insurance service providers claim to be running tax-compliant reinsurance pools. However, just as you cannot judge a book by its cover, you cannot assume that the service provider is running a reinsurance pool in compliance with IRS expectations. In examining any potential reinsurance pooling arrangement for your captive, you will want to obtain answers to these basic questions:

- *How many captives participate in your pool?* As noted previously, Revenue Ruling 2002-90 indicates that twelve *related* entities can satisfy risk distribution. Therefore, a pool with at least twelve *unrelated* captives should go a long way toward meeting this requirement. That said, you have to ask yourself if just meeting the bare minimum is good enough or frankly even a good idea. The more participants and the greater the diversity (industry, geography, risks), the better.

- *What is the pool's loss history?* This is a double-edged sword. On the one hand, you want to see that the pool has a history of losses. After all, a genuine reinsurance pool should expect to incur losses from year to year, and each of the participants in the pool should be expected to chip in toward reimbursing these losses. At the same time, you do not want your captive to join a reinsurance pool if the pool shows a history of large losses and a small number of participants. This would beg the question "what's the point?" If you are careful in managing the liabilities of your business in order to conserve insurance costs and keep claims to a minimum, then you should expect your fellow participants in the reinsurance pool to likewise manage their claims and minimize losses.
- *Are funds actually changing hands?* With the growing popularity of captive insurance companies, it still boggles my mind when I speak with captive managers and find out that they don't actually transfer funds but rather enter into an agreement based on constructive receipt. It is imperative that you can illustrate actual flows of funds between the participants of the reinsurance pooling facility.

- *Who are the other participants?* For years, my law firm would be engaged for the establishment of a client's captive and the ongoing legal and regulatory compliance. We would bring in third-party managers to actually handle the operational aspects of the captive, including the administration of the reinsurance pooling. However, it dawned on me one day that just because we established our captives appropriately and provided ongoing legal and regulatory oversight, we didn't actually know who the other pool participants were. For this reason alone, I formed Hamilton Captive Management. Sitting in law school, I never once thought about being a captive manager. So when I'm asked why I formed the management company, my response is always the same: out of necessity!

Step 5: Investing Captive Assets While Insurance Coverage Is in Effect

As I explained in chapter 1, the premiums paid into your captive insurance company become assets of the captive. It is the responsibility of the manager of your captive to see that these assets are soundly managed so that the captive can pay any claims that might be incurred in respect of any insurance issued to your business. With any luck, your claims will be low and your captive will be able to book the remaining assets as profits at the end of the coverage period of any insurance policies written with respect to those assets.

Most captive insurance companies provide a business plan to an insurance regulator when they are first licensed. The business plan informs the regulator how the captive will be operated, the types of policies that will be issued, the nature of any losses that may be incurred, and the investment activity that the captive intends to pursue. The insurance regulator will seek to determine that your captive prudently manages its assets to satisfy claims as they are incurred.

As you can imagine, an insurance regulator will not be impressed if the manager of your captive seeks to gamble the premium income of your captive on the blackjack tables in Las Vegas. Similarly, putting premium income into venture capital projects and other illiquid investments will jeopardize the ability of your captive to pay claims when they are incurred.

Most captive insurance company business plans call for the premium income of the captive insurance company to be invested conservatively while an insurance policy is in effect. Once the policy has expired and the premium income has been booked into profits, the business plan may permit your captive to engage in a less conservative manner. With that said, I would encourage you to continue to invest the surplus in a conservative manner.

Accordingly, your captive insurance company will be permitted to invest its premium income and capital into a broad array of investments that are largely conservative, with a greater focus on government bonds and other cash-based investments. Stocks and other investments may be limited to a designated percentage of your captive's investment portfolio during the time that insurance coverage is in place.

One great advantage of owning a captive insurance company is that you can have your investment advisor manage the assets of the captive, as mentioned in chapter 1. Many times, the assets of your captive can even be held with your investment advisor's firm. The manager of your captive will evaluate your investment advisor to ensure that the advisor is properly licensed, insured, and qualified to oversee the captive's investment portfolio. Once the investment advisor is approved to handle your captive's portfolio, the captive manager will provide your investment advisor with an investment mandate outlining the captive's investment requirements and any limitations imposed by the business plan or the insurance regulator. This document is typically referred to as an investment policy statement. Most SEC-registered investment advisors are familiar with this process and are prepared to work with an investment mandate, even if they have never managed the portfolio for a captive insurance company before. Furthermore, most major banks and brokerage firms in the United States will permit your captive to open an investment account and keep assets with them in the United States, even if the captive has been established in a foreign country.

Step 6: Investing Captive Assets Once Insurance Coverage Has Ended

As discussed in Step 5, once the premium received by your captive has been booked into profits, your investment advisor should enjoy greater flexibility to invest those profits (assuming that this is consistent with your expectations). After all, those profits are now yours (inside your captive insurance company) and do not need to be set aside to meet any claims once outside the coverage period.

One very important tax benefit of a captive, which chapter 2 covers in detail, is the dividends-received deduction. You may recall that your captive enjoys an exemption from tax for up to $2.2 million[8] of premium income each year. In addition, your captive gets to exempt 70 percent of its dividend income from regular stock investments. Another way of saying this is that your captive only incurs a tax liability of 30 percent of the normal corporate tax liability, which

8 | Effective January 1, 2017, changes to The PATH ACT, made in December 2015, increase the tax exemption for premiums paid from $1.2 to $2.2 million annually (adjusted for inflation).

ranges from 15 percent to 35 percent for most income brackets, meaning that your captive has an effective tax rate of between 4.2 percent and 10 percent on its dividend income.

In chapter 2, I cited the example of Alan, who holds GE stock inside his Bahamas-based captive's investment portfolio, and Craig, who holds GE stock in his personal portfolio. Because Alan's captive can claim the dividends-received deduction, it pays a federal tax of 4.2 percent—and no state income tax whatsoever—on the dividends from his GE stock, whereas Craig pays combined federal and state income taxes of *over ten times this amount.*

The effect of the dividends-received deduction is that you can invest in stocks much more tax efficiently using your captive than you can through your own personal portfolio. This generous tax exemption enables you to accumulate far greater wealth within your captive than you possibly can on your own. Consider this point: if your captive pays only 4.2 percent per year on $50,000 of dividends, you have $47,900 after taxes to reinvest. If instead you receive $50,000 of dividends in your own personal stock portfolio, in some states you may be taxed as high as 50 percent on those same dividends, meaning you have only $25,000 left after taxes to reinvest.

The difference in taxes in this example, $22,900, means that you almost double your money after taxes with a captive. Over ten years, that's almost a quarter of a million dollars in tax savings, and that is not even including the additional earnings you would accumulate by reinvesting those savings. In fact, if your captive earns just 6 percent per year on its investment portfolio, the cumulative savings over ten years is just over $300,000. Of course, when you finally pull this money out of your captive, you will incur a tax liability, but we discuss ways to mitigate the tax impact of that in the next step.

Step 7: Getting Your Money Out of the Captive

As discussed in the preceding step, your captive insurance company pays a lower rate of income tax on dividends than you do. This enables you to accumulate wealth inside your captive at a far greater clip than you can in your personally held investment portfolio. The reason is twofold: (1) your captive enjoys a dividends-received deduction against its federal income tax liability on qualified dividends, and (2) your captive is investing pretax dollars allowing for the compounding of assets at a faster rate.

If your captive performs as most captives do, it will accumulate wealth from a combination of strong claims management, prudent investment management, and more efficient taxation. This means that you will have a very good problem to consider: *How to extract all that wealth from inside your captive.*

Fortunately, there are many convenient, tax-efficient ways to access capital within your captive as well as to ultimately liquidate your captive in a tax-efficient manner. The following paragraphs discuss just a few of the ways that this can be done.

Shareholder Loans

Many corporations frequently lend funds to their shareholders. While the practice is common, the IRS has a long history of examining shareholder loans to ensure that such transactions are not devices to extract dividends from the lender corporation free of tax. In the context of captive insurance, the IRS frequently cites non-arm's length arrangements as indicia that the captive is not engaged in legitimate insurance activities.[9] Therefore, it is paramount that the captive stick to formalities when advancing shareholder loans.

A competent captive manager will evaluate the purpose of a shareholder loan and the financial ability of the shareholder to repay it. Most captive jurisdictions require that the captive's business plan expressly limit the amount of loans, including shareholder loans, that can comprise its asset base. Many regulators, and the captive managers they regulate, will also limit the scope and duration of a shareholder loan in order to ensure that funds are repaid in time to meet any catastrophic claims incurred by the captive.

Dividends

The most obvious way to extract accumulated wealth from your captive is to have the captive declare a dividend. Until 2013, owners of a captive enjoyed the same reduced federal income tax rate on qualified dividends as owners of any other corporation: 15 percent. Today, depending on a variety of factors, that rate generally is 15 to 20 percent. Please bear in mind that you may be subject to state income tax on those same dividends, and in certain states those dividend taxes may be as much as the federal income tax rate! Regardless, whether it is a 15 percent or 20 percent federal income tax rate, it still is not a bad deal when compared to ordinary income tax rates that can exceed 50 percent and customarily do.

Liquidating the Captive

Liquidating your captive should only be considered if (1) you are ineligible to enjoy a reduced tax rate on dividends received from

9 | See, e.g., FSA 200202002 (investment of 97.5 percent of a captive's assets with affiliated companies, and lack of formality in transactional documentation, cast doubt on the captive's capacity to pay insurance claims).

your captive or (2) you are certain that you won't need your captive to conduct any more insurance activities. After all, your captive insurance company represents a significant investment on your part. Once it is gone, you will again have to pay advisors and service companies to reinstate your captive or to form a new captive.

In a complete liquidation of your captive, the amount you receive from your captive in redemption of all the stock in your captive qualifies as a capital gain. If you have held your captive stock for more than a year, you may be able to enjoy a much lower "long-term" capital gains tax rate. Income tax rates are like tides—they rise and fall fairly regularly and typically when a new administration takes over Congress and the White House. Sometimes the changes are significant; sometimes they are not. The current long-term capital gains rate ranges from 15 percent to 20 percent for most taxpayers, depending on a variety of circumstances.

It is important to bear in mind that the capital gains tax incurred when you liquidate your captive is a singular event. As long as you keep your money inside your captive and do not take dividends, you do not incur any income tax as a shareholder of the captive. The captive itself pays federal income taxes on its earnings at corporate tax rates, but—as discussed earlier—qualified dividends received by your captive often qualify for a 70 percent dividends-received deduction.

Properly managed, your captive is a highly tax-efficient vehicle for holding investments until you decide that you no longer need the captive and want to liquidate it. When you liquidate your captive, you incur one single tax liability at the long-term capital gains tax rate on the proceeds received from your captive, less your tax basis in the stock you hold in your captive. Your tax basis in the stock of your captive insurance company includes the amounts you have invested as capital as well as legal fees and other expenses incurred when acquiring your stock in the captive.

Chapter Four

WHAT YOU NEED TO KNOW ABOUT MANAGING YOUR CAPTIVE INSURANCE COMPANY

Tax and Regulatory Requirements

Once you establish your own captive insurance company, you will quickly learn that there are a number of tax and regulatory requirements that apply. Failure to meet these requirements may result in the loss of a valuable tax deduction or even the loss of your captive's insurance license. Fortunately, most captive insurance managers arrange for these tax and regulatory obligations to be met. Nevertheless, you should become familiar with these requirements so that you can properly gauge whether your service provider is up to the job. Depending on the resources you have at your disposal, you may even desire to have your own attorneys and accountants help you to comply with these requirements.

By "tax requirements," we mean those requirements of US tax law that apply to your captive insurance company. Regulatory requirements are those requirements of local corporate and insurance law that apply to your captive. Because we have already touched on a number of tax law requirements in earlier chapters, we will first cover the important regulatory requirements that need to be met before discussing the tax requirements.

Key Regulatory Requirements

You will first experience important regulatory requirements when you set out to establish your captive insurance company. Practically all jurisdictions that offer captive insurance arrangements require that your captive be properly licensed and managed. In addition to a license application process that may require you to submit a significant amount of information about yourself and the insured business, you will be required to fund your captive with sufficient capital to meet the requirements of local law. The insurance regulator will also require that your captive engage the services of an experienced insurance manager approved by the regulator to operate captives. This is where a captive insurance service provider offering a comprehensive suite of services is crucial. Instead of you needing to recruit a qualified captive manager, CPA, registered agent, and auditor to help you run your captive, your captive manager will usually handle this task for you.

Once your captive insurance company is formed, your captive manager will likely be required by law to prepare an operations manual. Even in those jurisdictions that do not require such a manual, many experienced captive managers will prepare one anyway. The operations manual will outline all of the different filing and reporting requirements that apply to your captive, as well as the procedures that the captive undertakes to satisfy these reporting obligations. The typical filings that a captive insurance company must make with most insurance regulators include the filing of an annual financial statement that is audited by a firm approved by the regulator for this purpose.

Most jurisdictions that provide for the licensing of captives require that all captive insurance companies file audited financial statements on at least an annual basis. The insurance regulator will most likely examine these audited statements to determine whether your captive is meeting the financial requirements of its insurance license. If you have a standalone captive, the regulator may compare your captive's audited financial statements against the financial projects contained in the business plan filed with your captive's original insurance license application.

Reinsurance Requirements

Even if you satisfy the requirements of the insurance regulator in the jurisdiction where your captive is formed, your captive still has to meet the requirements of one other group of interested parties: reinsurance firms. Most captives rely on reinsurance pooling agreements to achieve the risk distribution that is required of them under US tax law. This means that your captive contractually joins with many other captives to share premiums and risks, spreading the economic impact of any one catastrophic risk among many members.

As you would expect, the reinsurance pool and its members will scrutinize your captive to ensure that in accepting you as a member they are not walking into catastrophic liabilities. A reinsurance pool is like a country club: it has members, and those members contractually commit to each other that they will pay the club's bills and keep the club running. Therefore, in accepting new members into the "club," the reinsurance pool seeks to confirm that (1) your captive will act prudently to keep claims low and (2) your captive will contribute financially if the pool suffers a catastrophic claim.

The management team for the reinsurance pool will examine the approach taken by the managers, underwriters, actuaries, and attorneys of your captive to issue policies to your business. They will want to see that your captive is prepared to manage claims conservatively so as to minimize losses and prevent the reinsurance pool from having to absorb large claims.

In this regard, your captive manager usually retains the services of an underwriter to help it issue insurance policies to your business on an annual basis. An underwriter normally assesses the risks of your business and reviews the potential impact that frequent or catastrophic claims may have on your captive. The underwriter then works with an actuary to determine what the captive should charge for the insurance coverage it offers your business, setting the terms of the policy, the policy limit, and the premium to be assessed.

The reinsurance pool's management team will thoroughly examine the activities of your captive's underwriters and actuaries to ensure compliance with underwriting requirements for pool members. The reinsurance pool will also want to ensure that the relationship between your captive and your business is an arm's length one and that transactions between your two entities are properly documented and effected at reasonable insurance prices. The reinsurance pool management and members depend on your captive to contribute toward catastrophic losses of the pool. Depending on the structure of the reinsurance pool, if your captive does not respect formalities and abide by its contractual obligations, the reinsurance pool may be left with an unpaid claim to be absorbed by its remaining members.

Management

In dealing with insurance regulators and with reinsurance pools, there are two very important aspects of managing your captive: financial management and claims management. Financial management encompasses the activities undertaken by your captive's directors and officers to ensure that your captive is managed prudently with respect to its finances. In addition to ensuring that the captive is adequately capitalized to absorb a catastrophic claim, sound financial management also requires that your captive price its insurance coverage appropriately and foster profits for long-term savings. Those profits need to be prudently managed by a capable investment advisor consulting with your captive's directors and officers to ensure they are acting within the bounds of the investment policy statement. Many captives have management teams that mirror what you would expect with any public insurance company: a chief financial officer or treasurer, a financial controller, in-house accounting team, auditors, and professional tax advisors. Captive insurance service providers often furnish these people and their functions through a management services agreement with your captive.

Claims management is equally important. After all, you do not prudently invest the money inside your captive only to have the captive pay out on a claim that could have been avoided. You may choose to have claims management conducted by your own staff within the captive, or you may opt to have a captive insurance service provider furnish this service through a management services agreement. It is significantly more common for the captive manager to handle the claims process. Deftly handled, the claims management team should negotiate on behalf of your captive to investigate claims fully and settle them on terms that are as favorable as possible for your captive. From time to time, your claims management team may even choose to litigate certain claims rather than paying them outright.

Tax Requirements

Your captive insurance company is a corporation. Like any other corporation, it may have an obligation to file returns and pay taxes in the United States. For a domestic captive, most likely returns will be filed at both the federal and state level. A foreign captive, on the other hand, has no tax reporting obligation under US income tax law unless you choose to do so. Nevertheless, it is likely in your interest to have your foreign captive elect to file returns and pay taxes as if it were a US carrier.

IRC § 953(d) Election

Why would you want to have your foreign captive file returns and pay taxes in the United States? You may recall from chapter 2 that IRC Section 831(b) permits your captive to exclude up to $2.2 million[10] in premium income each year. This election is only available for domestic insurance companies, since foreign insurance companies are not subject to federal income tax.

IRC Section 953(d) permits a foreign insurance company to file an election with the IRS to be taxed as if it were a domestic insurance company. The precise requirements of Section 953(d) exceed the scope of this book. However, the foreign captive must generally

10 | Effective January 1, 2017, changes to The PATH Act, made in December 2015, increase the tax exemption for premiums paid from $1.2 to $2.2 million annually (adjusted for inflation).

demonstrate to the IRS that it has US shareholders and a US bank account.

If a foreign captive fails to make this election, the captive itself remains free of US income tax, but the US shareholder of the foreign captive must then report the captive's income as "subpart F" income under the controlled foreign corporation rules of US tax law. In other words, the income of the foreign captive "passes through" to the US shareholder's income tax return, and the shareholder cannot claim the $2.2 million exclusion under Section 831(b). For this reason, most foreign captives elect under Section 953(d) to be taxed as domestic insurance companies, enabling themselves to secure the $2.2 million exemption under Section 831(b).

IRC § 831(b) Election

One of the key benefits of a captive insurance company is the ability to save up to $2.2 million each year free of income tax. In order to secure this benefit, your captive needs to file an election each year with the IRS to be taxed under an "alternative" regime.[11]

Both the 953(d) and 831(b) elections are critical to the success of your captive. Failure to properly make these elections on a timely basis can be costly for you and your business. For this reason, it is very important that you retain the services of a competent tax advisor who is experienced in handling tax filings for captive insurance companies. A qualified captive manager should actually handle the financial reporting and tax filings on your behalf and should work with your personal tax advisor to ensure all matters have been fully complied with.

11 | IRC § 831(b)(2)(A)(ii).

Filing and Payment Requirements

Each year, your captive needs to file IRS Form 1120-PC, which is the standard form of tax return for a property and casualty insurance company. The filing deadline is March 15th of each year, although your captive can request a six-month extension until September 15th in any given year. The first time that the captive files its tax return, the captive will most likely also make the 953(d) and 831(b) elections (depending on timing).

Because your captive is taxed as a corporation, it pays taxes like everyone else (albeit, $2.2 million in premium income is exempt from tax, and stock dividends enjoy a 70 percent dividends-received deduction). Your captive will be required to make quarterly estimated tax payments on April 15th, June 15th, September 15th, and December 15th each year. For foreign captives, the estimated tax payments should be made from the captive's domestic bank account.

Risk Shifting and Risk Distribution

We have touched on the two concepts of risk shifting and risk distribution at several points throughout the course of this book. Nevertheless, I wish to summarize for you these key concepts and the manner in which your captive must abide by these requirements. If your captive fails to meet these requirements, your business cannot deduct the premiums paid as insurance expenses, nor can your captive claim the benefits of the $2.2 million exclusion for insurance premium income.

Helvering v. Le Gierse[12] is the seminal US Supreme Court case that defines "insurance" for tax law purposes. The Supreme Court found that insurance features two fundamental elements: risk shifting

12 | 312 US 531 (1941).

and risk distribution. Earlier, I explained that "risk shifting" exists when risk is transferred from one party to another, such as when you enter into a contract of insurance. I also introduced you to the principle behind "risk distribution," wherein an insurance company pools risks from many different parties in order to achieve a statistical smoothing effect so that no one risk is so large as to bankrupt the insurance company.

You may recall from earlier in this book that the IRS initially disallowed premiums paid in captive insurance arrangements. The IRS took the view that any insurance transactions within the same economically interrelated group of companies lacked the risk shifting and risk distribution elements required under the Le Gierse case. However, no federal court ever accepted the "economic family" doctrine advocated by the IRS. Courts instead upheld captive insurance arrangements where risk shifting and risk distribution could be established.

The IRS ultimately conceded that captive insurance is a legitimate arrangement and, in Revenue Ruling 2001-31, acknowledged that businesses may deduct premiums paid to related captive insurance companies. As a result, pursuant to Revenue Ruling 2002-75, you can even apply for a ruling from the IRS blessing your captive arrangement. Because captive insurance is so popular, and the line of cases and rulings has so clearly defined the boundaries of permissible captive insurance activities, most captive owners do not find it necessary to obtain a ruling from the IRS.

As discussed in chapter 1, risk shifting is fairly easy to achieve. Most captives satisfy this requirement simply by issuing insurance policies and collecting premiums in return, thereby shifting the risk of liability from the insured business to the captive insurance company. Nevertheless, the IRS scrutinizes arrangements to ensure that the insurance arrangement involves a real transfer of risk. The IRS and federal courts will disallow a deduction if it can be established that risk was never really transferred and that the insured business retained all the risk.[13]

Following its change in position regarding captive insurance arrangements, the IRS issued a series of rulings to help define the outer limits of risk distribution. In Revenue Ruling 2002-89, it held that a captive insuring more than 50 percent of its total portfolio of risks with unrelated parties satisfied the risk distribution requirement, whereas a captive insuring more than 90 percent of its risk portfolio with its parent company lacked adequate risk distribution. In Revenue Ruling 2002-90, the IRS went even further by concluding that a captive insuring the risks of twelve related companies satisfied the risk distribution requirement; no more than 15 percent of its entire risk pool comprised the risks of any one of those twelve companies.

Revenue Ruling 2002-91 gives further definition to the IRS line of thought. In that ruling, a group captive consisting of seven members was designed so that no one member's risks would exceed 15 percent of the entire risk pool insured by the captive. Consistent with Revenue Ruling 2002-90, the IRS concluded that the group captive satisfied the risk distribution requirement. Accordingly, the culmination of IRS guidance suggests that related parties can help satisfy the risk distribution requirement, either as members of the same group of companies (Revenue Ruling 2002-90) or as co-owners of the same group captive (Revenue Ruling 2002-91).

The courts have created an even more generous set of guidelines for captives. The *Harper Group* case cited in chapter 2 gave approval to an arrangement in which a captive insurance company fulfilled the

13 | See, e.g., *Gulf Oil Corp. v. Commissioner*, 914 F.2d 396 (3rd Cir. 1990).

risk distribution requirement even though it only insured 29 percent of risks from unrelated parties. However, in my experience, it is far safer to stick with the guidelines published by the IRS. Based on the IRS rulings discussed in this chapter, *a good rule of thumb is that your captive should insure, at a minimum, 50 percent of its risks among at least twelve parties. Preferably, however, this number should be substantially larger, with diversification amongst the participants geographically, their respective industries, and the risk insured by each individual captive.*

Chapter Five

PROTECTING YOUR ASSETS FROM LAWSUITS WITH A CAPTIVE INSURANCE COMPANY

Cost is not the only reason to go offshore. There is another financial services industry that has enjoyed tremendous growth in many offshore jurisdictions over the past two decades: asset protection. In this chapter, I will briefly discuss what we mean by "asset protection," and then I will outline the prevailing strategies implemented by lawyers to help protect their clients' assets from the claims of unanticipated creditors. I will then cover the many ways that captive insurance works with an asset protection plan to preserve your wealth for you and your family.

What Is Asset Protection?

"Asset protection" is a term used to describe any number of techniques that preserve your wealth for you and your family, often to the exclusion of uninvited creditors and their claims. There is no one particular technique that in and of itself may be referred to as asset protection. However, all forms of asset protection generally derive from one governing principle: your creditors cannot take from you what you do not own.

If you are like most people, you get in your car every day and drive—to work, to run your errands, and to return home at the end of the day. In many cities around the United States, jury verdicts for killing or paralyzing someone in a car accident can be $5 million or more.

Most Americans don't really think about the consequences of a $5 million tort judgment. After all, you cannot get blood from a stone; if you do not have $5 million in the bank, most plaintiffs' lawyers will simply accept the limits of your auto insurance in an out-of-court settlement.

But what happens if you do have $5 million in the bank? As a lawyer, I have grown a rather thick skin when people compare my profession to sharks circling a bleeding victim. However, the unfortunate truth is that a plaintiff's lawyer will not settle for auto insurance policy limits if the lawyer knows that you have $5 million in the bank. Instead, you will be dragged into court and the lawyer will collect on that judgment by going after your assets: your home, cars, bank accounts, and even retirement accounts in certain instances.

Many people think that asset protection is something for the very wealthy, but the wealthiest Americans are somewhat immune to this problem. If you are a billionaire, your lifestyle will not be affected if you have to cut a check for $5 million. *Asset protection is of real value to those people who have worked all their lives and saved up a sum of money that, if lost as a result of a catastrophic liability, would affect their lifestyle.*

My example concerning auto liability applies universally, but it is not the only form of personal liability you face every day. America is a litigious nation, and each year we see an increasing number of lawsuits filed in courthouses all over the country. In addition to personal liabilities, you also face liabilities in your business.

Fortunately, there are planning techniques that can be applied to help shield your assets from a catastrophic liability. We use captive insurance, in part, to help address the problem of inadequate insurance in your business. *Asset protection, however, is really addressed at protecting you from inadequate insurance in your personal life.*

How Do You Protect Assets?

As I mentioned earlier, there is no single technique used to protect your assets from unanticipated claims. Depending on the type of assets you have, an asset protection lawyer may recommend one or more different planning strategies designed to protect particular assets. Furthermore, there is no magic bullet in asset protection planning: no single technique is absolutely foolproof. Depending on the nature of the claim, and the determination and resources of your creditor, asset protection planning might succeed, but there is a risk that it will not.

Asset protection planning employs any number of techniques to separate your assets from you so that you are in a position to claim that you do not own those assets if you are sued. As a lawyer, there are a number of devices I can structure for you to utilize that would separate you from your assets, much of which will depend on your comfort. Therefore, the asset protection lawyer often tries to find a happy medium between (1) your desire to have quick, convenient access to your assets and (2) the lawyer's mission to create as much distance as possible between you and your assets.

It is safe to say that, in general, an asset protection plan implemented before a creditor's claim arises stands the best chance of success. Usually, an asset protection lawyer will advise you to transfer your assets out of your name and into the name of a third party, typically someone who is relatively immune from litigation (such as a trustee of an offshore trust). This technique derives from the principle that a creditor cannot take from you what you don't own, and most asset protection techniques involve, in one form or another, titling assets out of your name. Unfortunately, some people wait until the creditor's claim arises before deciding to engage in asset protection planning. If you wait until it is too late, your creditor may be able to argue that a transfer of your assets to someone else is a fraudulent transfer, allowing that creditor to sue the transferee and get at the transferred assets.

Asset Protection Trusts

The foreign asset protection trust is the single most successful asset protection technique available today. Its success owes to the fact that (1) it is relatively inexpensive to establish and (2) it involves the least amount of disruption in your personal life.

Trusts have existed in English and American common law for centuries. Most people who own significant assets have hired an estate planning attorney at some stage in their lives to create a trust that avoids probate and provides for family members when one passes away. Oftentimes, these trust agreements will contain a provision referred to among lawyers as a "spendthrift clause." This clause helps to ensure that your assets pass to your heirs free from any claims of their creditors.

For example, if you have a daughter who is stuck in a bad marriage and is contemplating divorce, a spendthrift clause in a trust makes clear that the trustee can only pass assets of the trust to your daughter and not to her creditors. Thus, if she subsequently gets a divorce and is required to split assets or pay alimony to her husband, the spendthrift clause empowers the trustee to refuse to pay out to anyone but your daughter.

Courts in the United States have long recognized that you cannot protect yourself from your creditors by contributing your assets to a trust in which you are a beneficiary protected by a spendthrift clause. Judges regard this as void against public policy, and they will disregard the spendthrift clause when warranted to award the assets of your trust to your creditors.

In the late 1980s, the Cook Islands became the first country in the world to pass a law making clear that you can fund a spendthrift trust in which you are a beneficiary of your own trust. The Cook Islands International Trusts Act 1982 overturns existing case law in the United States and provides a degree of certainty in asset protection planning. By placing your assets in a Cook Islands asset protection trust before a creditor's claim arises, your assets are protected in most instances.

The asset protection trust can take many forms, but in most cases it is simply an irrevocable trust that functions in most ways like a standard revocable living trust used in estate planning. There is a person, known as the "trustee," who takes charge of your assets. As the grantor of your trust, you normally reserve special powers in the trust agreement that allow you to gain access to your trust assets when you are not being pursued by creditors. With foreign asset protection trusts, there is typically someone known as the "protector" who monitors the activities of the trustee and can replace the trustee when desired.

Since the Cook Islands first introduced its asset protection trust law, over a dozen other countries and numerous states have enacted asset protection trust legislation. It is now possible to establish an asset protection trust under the laws of Alaska, Delaware, Nevada, and South Dakota, to name a few states. Yet, foreign asset protection trusts are universally regarded as the gold standard among experienced practitioners for one very special reason: under the US Constitution, each state is required to give "full faith and credit" to the judgments rendered in every other state in the United States. This is referred to as the Full Faith and Credit Clause, and it means that a Nevada judge is powerless to protect your Nevada trust if a creditor in Iowa happens to get a judgment against your trustee in another state's court or in federal court.

A colleague of mine who is a partner at one of the best-known law firms in Nevada tells me that, as a result of the Full Faith and Credit Clause of the US Constitution, a Nevada asset protection trust is only effective if you are a Nevada resident and your creditor also happens to be a Nevada resident. With that type of uncertainty, it is little wonder that most asset protection lawyers prefer to set up trusts in a foreign jurisdiction that offers asset protection trust legislation.

Enjoying the Use of Assets Held within Your Foreign Asset Protection Trust

The foreign asset protection trust has become the most popular technique for asset protection planning because it is a perfect marriage between (1) asset protection effectiveness and (2) convenience for clients who want to enjoy access to the assets held within their trusts. Asset protection planning lawyers understand the efficacy of the foreign asset protection trust because of the case law precedent in the Cook Islands and other jurisdictions. Also, many cases involving foreign asset protection trusts have been fully litigated in the United States, and we can draw lessons from and conclusions about asset protection planning from these cases. Reduced to a simple principle, foreign asset protection trusts work better than any other known asset protection planning technique for most cases. As long as you establish and fund the trust while you are solvent and before you have any potential creditor issues, the assets within a properly structured foreign asset protection trust are protected for you and your family.

One of the most frequent questions I receive when discussing foreign asset protection trusts is "How do I access the money inside a foreign asset protection trust?" Surprisingly, for most people it is easier than you might expect. Most foreign asset protection trusts permit the grantor (the person who establishes and funds the trust) to direct the trustee to make gifts from the trust. The grantor may even make gifts from the trust through the grantor's will. This power is *limited*, meaning that you cannot exercise this power to make a gift to yourself, your creditor, or to someone else's creditor. Aside from this, however, there is generally no limitation on your ability to make gifts from your asset protection trust at any time.

One way that you can access the assets of your trust for yourself is to simply ask the trustee. The laws of many foreign jurisdictions, including Belize and the Cook Islands, permit you to be a beneficiary of your own spendthrift trust. You can name yourself as a beneficiary of your own trust and thereby periodically make requests of the trustee to distribute money to you as a beneficiary.

The simplest way that clients may control the assets of their foreign asset protection trust is to hold those assets in a business entity (such as your captive insurance company) that is owned by the trust. One very popular planning arrangement is for the foreign asset protection trust to own a domestic or foreign limited liability company (LLC) managed by the client. As manager of the LLC, you can direct the activities of the LLC, including its investments, and pay yourself a salary. You can even borrow from the LLC. At the same time, because the LLC is owned by your foreign asset protection trust, your assets remain protected from the claims of unanticipated creditors. Of course, the precise structure and mechanics exceed the scope of this book, and you will want to discuss this planning technique with an asset protection lawyer.

It's important to keep in mind that just because a foreign asset protection trust creates a degree of separation between you and your assets does not mean that you have to give up all access to, and control of, your assets. Rather, properly structured, you should continue to enjoy convenient access to, and control of, the assets of your foreign asset protection trust while securing an extremely high degree of protection against unanticipated creditors. There is simply no more effective, cost-efficient technique available for protecting your assets than the foreign asset protection trust.

Income Tax Aspects of the Foreign Asset Protection Trust

Whenever a US person forms a trust, including a foreign trust, the trust is most often regarded as a "grantor trust" for US income tax purposes. (This discussion pertains to *income* taxes as opposed to *estate* taxes.) This means that all of the income and activities of your foreign asset protection trust flow through to your personal income tax return each year. It is as if your trust does not exist for tax purposes, even though the trust is very real for legal and asset protection purposes.

If your trust owns an underlying entity, such as a limited liability company, you can arrange it so that the LLC is also a pass-through for income tax purposes. By default, a domestic LLC owned entirely by your foreign asset protection trust enjoys pass-through status. A foreign LLC, such as one formed in Nevis or the Cook Islands, can qualify for pass-through status, but you must first file an election with the IRS to this effect. This way, having a foreign asset protection trust along with a foreign LLC keeps your tax reporting simple and straightforward: everything gets reported on your personal income tax return.

There are some additional filing requirements to be mindful of. For this reason, I highly recommend that you engage the services of a qualified CPA whenever you consider setting up a foreign asset protection trust. By "qualified," I mean a CPA who regularly prepares information and tax returns for clients who have foreign asset protection trusts. You do not want to engage a CPA who has never done this before, as some of these filing requirements come with very strict penalties if the returns are not properly completed and timely filed.

Fraudulent Transfers

If you do not fund your trust before a creditor's claim arises, or if it can be proven that you intended to avoid your creditor by establishing the trust, the laws of most jurisdictions, including the Cook Islands, permit the creditor to set aside the transfer as a fraudulent transfer. You should be aware that the term "fraudulent" here is a civil matter and not a criminal one. If the creditor establishes that you transferred your assets at a time when you were insolvent, or you transferred assets with the intent to delay, hinder, or defraud your creditor, in most jurisdictions the creditor can sue the transferee as well as try to regain custody of the assets. Fortunately, the laws of the Cook Islands and many other leading asset protection trust jurisdictions make it much more difficult for a creditor to prove the existence of a fraudulent transfer, and many offshore jurisdictions severely limit the creditor's remedies.

Since the Cook Islands first passed asset protection trust legislation, at least a dozen other countries have passed similar laws, including Nevis and Belize. In fact, Belize has surpassed the Cook Islands as a leading asset protection trust jurisdiction by clarifying that there are no circumstances in which a creditor can gain access to assets of a Belize asset protection trust. Simply put, once you fund a Belize asset protection trust, you and the beneficiaries of your trust are the only people who will ever have access to the assets of your trust.

How Does Captive Insurance Protect Your Assets?

One of the key benefits of captive insurance is that by paying an insurance premium, you transfer excess cash from your business into a captive insurance company. Over time, the savings accumulated inside a captive should be quite substantial. Because this money is owned by your captive, and not held in your own name, it is not readily available to your creditors if you are sued.

While assets of a captive insurance company are technically only available to pay the claims of the insured, the problem is that if your captive is based in Vermont, Delaware, Tennessee, or any other domestic jurisdiction, it is possible for the creditor to obtain a court order compelling you to disgorge the assets of your captive to satisfy a judgment. How about using a foreign domicile for your captive's licensure? Many jurisdictions offer special rules protecting the assets held within a captive. *For asset protection reasons, foreign captives tend to be much safer than domestic captives.* In fact, domestic captives offer far less asset protection benefit.

As you may expect from the preceding discussion on foreign asset protection trusts, in the right circumstance, many lawyers advise their clients to use such a trust to own the captive insurance company provided there are no PATH Act issues with regard to the relatedness test. (Again, as discussed in chapter 1, the relatedness test, which applies to spouses and lineal descendants, requires that owners of the insured business own a share of the business equal to or greater than their ownership in the captive.)

The benefit of this technique is that, if properly structured, your creditor cannot require you to disgorge the investment assets of your captive insurance company. Instead, your creditor will be required to proceed against the foreign trustee under the laws of a jurisdiction that will likely dismiss all but the most egregious of lawsuits. Even then, the laws of most foreign asset protection trust-friendly jurisdictions do not permit creditors to bring claims for punitive damages, civil fines, or tort claims that are not recognized under the laws of that particular foreign country.

By using a captive insurance company domiciled offshore, you can protect your hard-earned wealth from lawsuits. At the same time, you will find that you enjoy tremendous flexibility to manage the investments and access the cash within your captive for your own needs. If I could obtain this result for you with a domestic captive, I would recommend it. *Unfortunately, assets held within a domestic captive are not safe from lawsuits, and you will be required to disgorge these assets if you suffer a judgment and have no other means to pay your creditor.*

There is one more key asset protection benefit of a captive insurance company: transferring wealth from your business (which has higher risks of catastrophic loss) to an offshore asset protection vehicle (which has lower risks of catastrophic loss). A few pages ago,

I described the problem of a fraudulent transfer: if you transfer assets when you are insolvent, or to intentionally avoid your creditor, even a foreign court may permit your creditor to have the transfer set aside.

One common exception to the rule on fraudulent transfers is that transfers for equivalent value are much more difficult for a creditor to challenge as a "fraudulent transfer." For example, if you were injured in a car accident and went to an emergency room for care, when you pay for the treatment provided, you have not engaged in a fraudulent transfer. You are injured, pay for medical care, and are not intentionally hindering, delaying, or defrauding a creditor by paying for a service provided for your general well-being.

The captive insurance company allows you to engage in this precise manner. Your business uses some of its excess cash to purchase insurance, thereby converting that cash into a policy that, in most instances, the creditor cannot lay claim to. For tax reasons, it is very important that the amount paid by your business for the insurance offered by your captive occur at arm's length, fair market prices. This same reason applies when analyzing the transaction from a fraudulent transfer perspective: as long as your business pays a fair price for the insurance offered by your captive, your creditor cannot pursue the captive on the grounds that the captive engaged in a sham transaction to defeat collection by your creditor.

Accordingly, the two key asset protection benefits of utilizing captive insurance are as follows:

1. By properly utilizing a foreign asset protection trust to hold the shares of stock in your offshore captive insurance company, your personal creditors cannot reach the assets of your captive.

2. Payments of premiums from your business to your captive for insurance coverage that is fairly priced cannot be set aside as fraudulent transfers. You therefore transfer assets from a structure that has higher risk (your business) to a structure that has lower risk (your offshore captive).

It is important to bear in mind that with most things in life and in business, timing is everything. If you wait until you are sued before visiting an asset protection lawyer, most likely you will not be able to protect your assets, including your captive, from being vulnerable to collection. *The ideal time for implementing an asset protection plan involving your captive is when you first seek to establish your captive.* Properly structured, you will sleep better at night knowing that the benefits of a lifetime of hard work and prudent savings are protected from the lawsuit lottery plaguing the nation.

Resources

IS A CAPTIVE INSURANCE COMPANY RIGHT FOR YOU?

Visit **www.thestrausslawfirm.com** to learn more about the professional services we offer our clients, including the proper formation and implementation of a captive insurance company. You can meet members of the team, learn about our history and mission, and hear about recent trends, news, and information regarding The Strauss Law Firm, LLC. You can also see where we may be educating audiences at any number of up-and-coming conferences and industry seminars. If you are interested, you are always invited to start a conversation.

Visit **www.hamiltoncaptivemanagement.com** to learn more about the day-to-day management services offered to our captive insurance company owners. Team members are profiled and their accomplishments can be read about from time to time in the News and Noteworthy pages. What was born out of necessity has formed the basis of a world-class organization. You will find that Hamilton Captive Management, LLC, provides clients with a full suite of solutions and a service that is unrivaled. The website is user-friendly and easy to navigate. Of course, you can also reach out to start a conversation with us as well.

Meet the author at **www.peterjstrauss.com**. We would welcome the opportunity to share additional reading materials including both books and articles written by Peter J. Strauss, JD, LL.M. If you are interested in attending a speech, workshop, or even webinar, you will find a number of up-to-date calendar events to choose from. Additionally, Mr. Strauss is also available for speaking engagements, educational seminars, and consulting projects. These can be custom-tailored for your industry, audience, or even organization. You can also follow him on LinkedIn, Twitter, and Instagram.

Take the quiz! In less than ten minutes you can complete this free online assessment. Once completed and submitted, you'll receive the answers you need to know in order to make an informed decision as to whether a captive insurance company may be right for you. The quiz can be found at **www.peterjstrauss.com**. Additionally, you'll receive the roadmap to forming your own insurance company.

Appendix

CAPTIVE INSURANCE CASES AND RULINGS

The following federal court cases and IRS rulings are referenced throughout this book. To assist you in your research on captive insurance, I thought it might be helpful to include a copy of these authorities in the back of this book.

1. *Helvering v. Le Gierse*, 312 US 531 (1941): In this case, the US Supreme Court introduces us to the concepts of "risk shifting" and "risk distribution" as required elements of "insurance" for tax purposes.

2. *Humana Inc. v. Commissioner*, 881 F.2d 247 (6th Cir. 1989): The Sixth Circuit Court of Appeals, ruling against the IRS, finds that a captive insurance company achieves sufficient risk distribution by insuring risks of multiple entities, notwithstanding that the entities are all related subsidiaries of a common corporate parent.

3. *Harper Group v. Commissioner*, 979 F.2d 1341 (9th Cir. 1992): Sufficient risk distribution exists even if the captive

only insures between 29 percent and 33 percent unrelated party risks.

4. Revenue Ruling 77-316: In this old IRS ruling, the Service indicates that it will disallow deductions of insurance premiums paid to a captive insurance company under "economic family" doctrine.

5. Revenue Ruling 2001-31: This is the seminal ruling in which the IRS announces that it will no longer disallow deductions of insurance premiums paid to a captive insurance company under the "economic family" doctrine.

6. Revenue Ruling 2002-89: This ruling contains a set of examples indicating that, for sufficient risk distribution to exist, the captive insurance company must not insure more than 50 percent unrelated party risks. The ruling also alludes to reinsurance pooling as a means of satisfying the risk distribution requirement.

7. Revenue Ruling 2002-90: A captive insurance company insures the risks of twelve subsidiaries of a common parent holding company. Conceding the issue in the *Humana* court decision, the IRS rules that sufficient risk distribution exists even though all the insured parties are related.

1. Helvering v. Le Gierse, 312 US 531 (1941):
US Supreme Court
No. 237
Argued January 9, 10, 1941
Decided March 3, 1941
312 US 531

CERTIORARI TO THE CIRCUIT COURT OF APPEALS FOR THE SECOND CIRCUIT

Syllabus

1. Within the meaning of § 302(g) of the Revenue Act of 1926, as amended, amounts "receivable as insurance" are amounts receivable as the result of transactions which involved, at the time of their execution, an actual insurance risk. P. 312 US 537.

2. Risk shifting and risk distribution are essentials of a contract of life insurance. P. 312 US 539.

3. A contract in the standard form of a life insurance policy, containing the usual provisions, including those for assignment or surrender, was issued to a woman of eighty years of age, without physical examination, for a single premium less than the face of the policy, together with an annuity policy for another premium calling for annual payments to her until her death. Although both policies were, on the face, separate contracts, neither referring to the other, and each was treated as independent in the matters of application, computation of premium, report and book entry of premium payment, maintenance of reserve, etc., they were issued at the same time, and the making of the annuity contract was a condition to the issuance of the life policy, and the combined effect was such that, in case of premature death,

the gain to the insurance company under one would neutralize its loss under the other.

Held:

(1) That the contracts must be considered together. P. 312 US 540.

(2) They created no insurance risk. P. 312 US 541.

[532]

Any risk that the prepayment would earn less than the amount paid by the insurance company as an annuity was an investment risk, not an insurance risk.

(3) The amount payable to the beneficiary named in the life policy, upon the death of the "insured," was not in the scope of § 302(g), *supra,* but was properly taxed in the decedent's estate under § 302(c) as a transfer to take effect in possession or enjoyment at or after death. P. 312 US 542.

110 F.2d 734 reversed.

Certiorari, 311 US 625, to review the affirmance of a decision of the Board of Tax Appeals, 39 B.T.A. 1134, reversing a deficiency assessment of estate tax.

[536]

MR. JUSTICE MURPHY delivered the opinion of the Court.

Less than a month before her death in 1936, decedent, at the age of 80, executed two contracts with the Connecticut General Life Insurance Co. One was an annuity contract in standard form entitling decedent to annual payments of $589.80 as long as she lived. The consideration stated for this contract was $4,179. The other contract was called a "Single Premium Life Policy-Non Participating" and provided for a payment of $25,000 to decedent's daughter, respondent Le Gierse at decedent's death. The premium specified was $22,946. Decedent paid the total consideration, $27,125 at the [537] time the contracts were executed. She was not required to pass a physical examination or to answer the questions a woman applicant normally must answer.

The "insurance" policy would not have been issued without the annuity contract, but, in all formal respects, the two were treated as distinct transactions. Neither contract referred to the other. Independent applications were filed for each. Neither premium was computed with reference to the other. Premium payments were reported separately and entered in different accounts on the company's books. Separate reserves were maintained for insurance and annuities. Each contract was in standard form. The "insurance" policy contained the usual provisions for surrender, assignment, optional modes of settlement, etc.

Upon decedent's death, the face value of the "insurance" contract became payable to respondent Le Gierse, the beneficiary. Thereafter, a federal estate tax return was filed which excluded from decedent's gross estate the proceeds of the "insurance" policy. The Commissioner notified respondents Bankers Trust Co. and Le Gierse, as executors of decedent's estate, that he proposed to include the proceeds of this policy in the gross estate, and to assess a deficiency. Suit in the Board of Tax Appeals followed, and the Commissioner's action was reversed. 39 B.T.A. 1134. The Circuit Court of Appeals affirmed. 110 F.2d 734. We brought the case here because of conflict with Commissioner v. Keller's Estate, 113 F.2d 833, and Helvering v. Tyler, 111 F.2d 422. 311 US 625.

The ultimate question is whether the "insurance" proceeds may be included in decedent's gross estate.

Section 302 of the Revenue Act of 1926, 44 Stat. 9, 70, as amended, 47 Stat. 169, 279, 48 Stat. 680, 752, provides:

"The value of the gross estate of the decedent shall be determined by including the value at the time [538] of his death of all property, real or personal, tangible or intangible . . ."

"* * * *"

"(g) To the extent of the amount receivable by the executor as insurance under policies taken out by the decedent upon his own life, and to the extent of the excess over $40,000 of the amount receivable by all other beneficiaries as insurance under policies taken out by the decedent upon his own life."

Thus, the basic question is whether the amounts received here are amounts "receivable as insurance" within the meaning of § 302(g).

Conventional aids to construction are of little assistance here. Section 302(g) first appeared in identical language in the Revenue Act of 1918 as § 402(f). 40 Stat. 1057, 1098. It has never been changed. [Footnote 1] None of the acts has ever defined "insurance." Treasury Regulations, interpreting the original provision, stated simply:

"The term 'insurance' refers to life insurance of every description, including death benefits paid by fraternal beneficial societies, operating under the lodge system."

Treasury Regulations No. 37, 1921 edition, p. 23. This statement has never been amplified. [Footnote 2] The committee report accompanying the Revenue Act of 1918 merely noted that the provision taxing insurance receivable by the executor clarified existing law, and that the provision taxing insurance in excess of $40,000 receivable by specific beneficiaries was inserted to prevent tax evasion. House Report No. 767, 65th Cong., 2d Sess., p. 22. [Footnote 3] Subsequent [539] committee reports do not mention § 302(g). Transcripts of committee hearings in 1918 and since are equally uninformative. [Footnote 4]

Necessarily, then, the language and the apparent purpose of § 302(g) are virtually the only bases for determining what Congress intended to bring within the scope of the phrase "receivable as insurance." In fact, in using the term "insurance," Congress has identified the characteristic that determines what transactions are entitled to the partial exemption of § 302(g).

We think the fair import of subsection (g) is that the amounts must be received as the result of a transaction which involved an actual "insurance risk" at the time the transaction was executed. Historically and commonly, insurance involves risk shifting and risk distributing. That life insurance is desirable from an economic and social standpoint as a device to shift and distribute risk of loss from premature death is unquestionable. That these elements of risk shifting and risk distributing are essential to a life insurance contract is agreed by courts and commentators. See, for example, Ritter v. Mutual Life Ins. Co., 169 US 139; In re Walsh, 19 F.Supp. 567; Guaranty Trust Co. v. Commissioner, 16 B.T.A. 314; Ackerman v. Commissioner, 15 B.T.A. 635; Couch, Cyclopedia of Insurance, Vol. I, § 61; Vance, [540] Insurance, §§ 1-3; Cooley, Briefs on Insurance, 2d edition, Vol. I, p. 114; Huebner, Life Insurance, Ch. 1. Accordingly, it is logical to assume that, when Congress used the words "receivable as insurance" in § 302(g), it contemplated amounts received pursuant to a transaction possessing these features. Commissioner v. Keller, supra; Helvering v. Tyler, supra; Old Colony Trust Co. v. Commissioner, 102 F.2d 380; Ackerman v. Commissioner, supra.

Analysis of the apparent purpose of the partial exemption granted in § 302(g) strengthens the assumption that Congress used the word "insurance" in its commonly accepted sense. Implicit in this provision is acknowledgement of the fact that, usually, insurance payable to specific beneficiaries is designed to shift to a group of individuals the risk of premature death of the one upon whom the beneficiaries are dependent for support. Indeed, the pith of the exemption is particular protection of contracts and their proceeds intended to guard against just such a risk. See Commissioner v. Keller, supra; United States Trust Co. v. Sears, 29 F.Supp. 643; Hughes, Federal Death Tax, p. 91; Comment, 38 Mich.L.Rev. 526, 528; compare Chase National Bank v. United States, 28 F.Supp. 947; In re Walsh, supra; Moskowitz v. Davis, 68 F.2d 818. Hence, the next question is whether the transaction in suit in fact involved an "insurance risk" as outlined above.

We cannot find such an insurance risk in the contracts between decedent and the insurance company.

The two contracts must be considered together. To say they are distinct transactions is to ignore actuality, for it is conceded on all sides, and was found as a fact by the Board of Tax Appeals, that the "insurance" policy would not have been issued without the annuity contract. Failure, even studious failure, in one contract to refer to the other cannot be controlling. Moreover, [541] authority for such consideration is not wanting, however unrealistic the distinction between form and substance may be. Commissioner v. Keller, supra; Helvering v. Tyler, supra. *See* Williston, Contracts, Vol. III, § 628; Paul, Studies in Federal Taxation, 2d series, p. 218; compare Pearson v. McGraw, 308 US 313. [Footnote 5]

Considered together, the contracts wholly fail to spell out any element of insurance risk. It is true that the "insurance" contract looks like an insurance policy, contains all the usual provisions of one, and could have been assigned or surrendered without the annuity. Certainly the mere presence of the customary provisions does not create risk, and the fact that the policy could have been assigned is immaterial, since, no matter who held the policy and the annuity, the two contracts, relating to the life of the one to whom they were originally issued, still counteracted each other. It may well be true that, if enough people of decedent's age wanted such a policy, it would be issued without the annuity, or that, if the instant policy had been surrendered, a risk would have arisen. In either event, the essential relation between the two parties would be different from what it is here. The fact remains that annuity and insurance are opposites; in this combination, the one neutralizes the risk customarily inherent in the other. From the company's viewpoint, insurance looks to longevity, annuity to transiency. See Commissioner v. Keller, supra; Helvering v. Tyler, supra; Old Colony Trust Co. v. Commissioner, supra; Carroll v. Equitable Life Assur. Soc., 9 F.Supp. 223; Note, 49 Yale L.J. 946; Cohen, Annuities and Transfer Taxes, 7 Kan.B.A.J. 139.

[542]

Here, the total consideration was prepaid, and exceeded the face value of the "insurance" policy. The excess financed loading and other incidental charges. Any risk that the prepayment would earn less than the amount paid to respondent as an annuity was an investment risk similar to the risk assumed by a bank; it was not an insurance risk as explained above. It follows that the sums payable to a specific beneficiary here are not within the scope of § 302(g). The only remaining question is whether they are taxable.

We hold that they are taxable under § 302(c) of the Revenue Act of 1926, as amended, as a transfer to take effect in possession or enjoyment at or after death. See Helvering v. Tyler, supra; Old Colony Trust Co. v. Commissioner, supra; Kernochan v. United States, 29 F.Supp. 860; Guaranty Trust Co. v. Commissioner, supra; compare Gaither v. Miles, 268 F. 692; Comment, 38 Mich.L.Rev. 526; Comment, 32 Ill.L.Rev. 223.

The judgment of the Circuit Court of Appeals is

Reversed.

THE CHIEF JUSTICE and MR. JUSTICE ROBERTS think the judgment should be affirmed for the reasons stated in the opinion of the Circuit Court of Appeals.

[Footnote 1]

Act of 1921; 42 Stat. 227, 279, § 402(f); Act of 1924; 43 Stat. 253, 305, § 302(g); Act of 1926; 44 Stat. 9, 71, § 302(g); Code of 1939; 53 Stat. 1, 122.

[Footnote 2]

Regulations No. 63, p. 26; Regulations No. 68, p. 31; Regulations No. 70, 1926 edition, p. 30; Regulations No. 70, 1929 edition, p. 33; Regulations No. 80, p. 62.

[Footnote 3]

". . . [Insurance payable to specific beneficiaries does] not fall within the existing provisions defining gross estate. It has been brought to the attention of the committee that wealthy persons have and now anticipate resorting to this method of defeating the estate tax. Agents of insurance companies have openly urged persons of wealth to take out additional insurance payable to specific beneficiaries for the reason that such insurance would not be included in the gross estate. A liberal exemption of $40,000 has been included, and it seems not unreasonable to require the inclusion of amounts in excess of this sum."

Id., p. 22. The same comment appears in Senate Report No. 617, 65th Cong., 3d Sess., p. 42.

[Footnote 4]

The curious consistency and inadequacy of section 302(g) have not escaped notice. See Paul, Life Insurance and The Federal Estate Tax, 52 Har.L.Rev. 1037; Paul, Studies in Federal Taxation, 3d Series, p. 351; United States Trust Co. v. Sears, 29 F.Supp. 643, 650.

[Footnote 5]

Legg v. St. John, 296 US 489, is not to the contrary. There, nothing indicated that the one contract would not have been issued without the other; there was no necessary connection between the two.

2. Humana Inc. v. Commissioner, 881 F.2d 247 (6th Cir. 1989): 881 F.2d 247

Humana Inc., Petitioner-appellant, v. Commissioner of Internal Revenue, Respondent-appellee

United States Court of Appeals, Sixth Circuit.--881 F.2d 247

Argued March 20, 1989. Decided July 27, 1989.

Laramie L. Leatherman, Charles J. Lavelle, James E. Milliman (argued), Greenebaum, Doll & McDonald, Louisville, KY., for petitioner-appellant.

Kenneth L. Greene (argued), David I. Pincus, US Dept. of Justice, Tax Div. Appellate Section, Washington, D.C., Gary R. Allen, Acting Chief, William S. Rose, Jr., Asst. Atty. Gen., Dept. of Justice, Tax Div., Washington, D.C., for respondent-appellee.

Before MARTIN and MILBURN, Circuit Judges, and HACKETT,* District Judge.

BOYCE F. MARTIN, Jr., Circuit Judge.

1

Humana Inc. and its wholly owned subsidiaries with which it files a consolidated federal income tax return appeal the decision of the United States Tax Court determining deficiencies against them with respect to their 1976-1979 fiscal years on the basis that: 1) sums paid by Humana Inc. to its captive insurance subsidiary, Health Care Indemnity, on its own behalf and on behalf of other wholly owned subsidiaries did not constitute deductible insurance premiums under the Internal Revenue Code Sec. 162(a) (1954), and 2) such payments are not deductible under the Internal Revenue Code Sec. 162 (1954) as ordinary and necessary business expenses as payments to a captive insurance company are equivalent to additions to a reserve for losses.

2

Humana Inc. and its subsidiaries operate hospitals whose insurance coverage was cancelled. Humana Inc. incorporated Health Care Indemnity, Inc., as a Colorado captive insurance company. In order to facilitate the incorporation of Health Care Indemnity, Humana Inc. also incorporated Humana Holdings, N.V., as a wholly owned subsidiary in the Netherlands Antilles. The only business purpose of Humana Holdings was to assist in the capitalization of Health Care Indemnity.[1] At the time of the initial capitalization, Health Care Indemnity issued 150,000 shares of preferred stock and 250,000 shares of common stock. Of these, Humana Holdings, the wholly owned Netherlands subsidiary, purchased the preferred stock for $250,000.00 in cash (its entire capitalization) and Humana Inc. purchased 150,000 shares of Health Care Indemnity's common stock for $750,000.00 in the form of irrevocable letters of credit (as provided by Colorado statute).

3

Health Care Indemnity, the captive insurance subsidiary of Humana Inc., provided insurance coverage for Humana Inc. and its other subsidiaries. Humana Inc. paid to Health Care Indemnity amounts which it treated as insurance premiums. Humana Inc. allocated and charged to the subsidiaries portions of the amounts paid representing the share each bore for the hospitals each operated. The remainder represented Humana Inc.'s share for the hospitals which it operated. The total sums, $21,055,575.00, were deducted on a consolidated income tax return as insurance premiums.

4

The Commissioner, in accordance with the position outlined in Rev. Rul. 77-316, 1977-2 C.B. 52, disallowed the deductions and asserted deficiencies against Humana Inc. and the subsidiaries. Humana Inc. and its subsidiaries filed petitions in the tax court for redeterminations of the deficiencies assessed against them. On August 14, 1985, the tax court issued a memorandum opinion upholding the Commissioner's determination. Following a petition for reconsideration, the tax court withdrew that opinion. Humana Inc. requested full court review. On January 26, 1987, the tax court, after review by the entire nineteen member court, upheld the Commissioner. Humana Inc. and Subsidiaries v. Commissioner, 88 T.C. 197 (1987).

5

The opinion of the tax court contains a twelve member majority written by Judge Goffe, an eight member concurrence written by Judge Whitaker and joined by seven members of the majority, a two member concurring opinion written by Judge Hamblen and joined by Judge Whitaker, and a seven member dissent written by Judge Korner. The twelve member majority relied on its prior decisions in Carnation Company v. Commissioner, 71 T.C. 400 (1978), aff'd. 640 F.2d 1010 (9th Cir.1981), cert. denied, 454 US 965, 102 S.Ct. 506, 70 L.Ed.2d 381 (1981) and Clougherty Packing Company v. Commissioner, 84 T.C. 948 (1985), aff'd. 811 F.2d 1297 (9th Cir.1987), and held 1) that sums paid by Humana Inc. to Health Care Indemnity on its own behalf (described as the "parent-subsidiary" issue) were not deductible as ordinary and necessary business expenses for insurance premiums, and 2) the sums charged by Humana Inc. to the operating subsidiaries (described as the "brother-sister" issue) were also not deductible on the consolidated income tax return as ordinary and necessary business expenses for insurance premiums. The majority reasoned that there was no insurance because the risks of loss were not shifted from Humana Inc. and its subsidiaries to Health Care Indemnity. In so holding, the majority specifically rejected adoption of the economic family concept argued by the Commissioner.

6

The tax court noted that the second issue, the brother-sister issue--whether the sums charged by Humana Inc. to its operating subsidiaries were deductible on the consolidated income tax returns as ordinary and necessary business expenses as insurance premiums--was an issue of first impression before the court. The court claimed that the issue had been decided in favor of denying the premiums as deductible in two other cases, Stearns-Roger Corp. v. United States, 774 F.2d 414 (10th Cir.1985) and Mobil Oil Corp. v. United States, 8 Cl.Ct. 555 (1985). The majority stated that Stearns-Roger and Mobil extended the rationale of Carnation and Clougherty to the "brother-sister" factual pattern. In holding that Humana Inc. did not shift the risk from the subsidiaries to Health Care Indemnity by charging its subsidiaries portions of the amounts paid representing the share each bore for the hospitals each operated, the tax court accepted the joint opinion of two experts, Dr. Plotkin and Mr. Stewart. Dr. Plotkin and Mr. Stewart stated:

7

Commercial insurance is a mechanism for transferring the financial uncertainty arising from pure risks faced by one firm to another in exchange for an insurance premium.... The essential element of an insurance transaction from the standpoint of the insured (e.g. Humana and its hospital network), is that no matter what perils occur, the financial consequences are known in advance.... A firm placing its risk in a captive insurance company in which it holds a sole ... ownership position, is not relieving itself of financial uncertainty.... True insurance relieves the firm's balance sheet of any potential impact of the financial consequences of the insured peril.... [However] as long as the firm deals with its captive, its balance sheet cannot be protected from the financial vicissitudes of the insured peril.

8

Humana, 88 T.C. at 219-25 (1987).

9

The majority also declared that payments to a captive insurance company are equivalent to additions to a reserve for losses and, therefore, not deductible under the Internal Revenue Code Sec. 162 (1954) as ordinary and necessary business expenses paid or incurred during the taxable years in issue. Stearns-Roger Corp. v. United States, 774 F.2d 414 (10th Cir.1985); Mobil Oil Corp. v. United States, 8 Cl.Ct. 555 (1985).

10

The eight-member concurrence agreed with the majority's conclusion on both issues but felt uncomfortable with the majority's reliance on the expert witnesses, Dr. Plotkin and Mr. Stewart, whose theories rested heavily upon the economic family concept of captive insurance companies. They wrote to affirm that they were holding against Humana solely on the basis that the contracts between Humana Inc. and Health Care Indemnity and the contracts between Humana Inc.'s subsidiaries and Health Care Indemnity were not insurance contracts because of the lack of risk shifting. Humana, 88 T.C. at 231 (1987) (Whitaker, J., concurring).

11

A two-member concurrence wrote to express concern about the "economic family" concept. They noted that the Commissioner's discussions of the economic family concept did not square with Moline Properties v. Commissioner, 319 US 436, 63 S.Ct. 1132, 87 L.Ed. 1499 (1943). The Supreme Court in Moline Properties held that each corporate taxpayer was a separate entity for tax purposes. The two-person concurrence felt that the Moline Properties issue was injected unnecessarily by way of the economic family concept analogy. The two-member concurrence noted that the majority cites proponents of the economic family concept and felt that this was neither appropriate nor necessary. The two-member concurrence stated that they "strongly believe that we should decide the issue solely on a lack of risk shifting and risk distribution basis." Humana, 88 T.C. at 237 (1987) (Hamblen, J., concurring).

12

The seven-member dissent concurred in part with the majority that the premiums paid to Health Care Indemnity by Humana Inc. for insurance on itself may not be deducted as insurance premiums. They dissented with respect to the majority's holding that the same result applies to premiums paid by Humana Inc.'s subsidiaries to Health Care Indemnity for comparable insurance on them and their employees. The dissent stated that neither Carnation nor Clougherty decided the issue of deductibility of insurance premiums where the insurance contract was between corporations related as brother and sister. The dissent stated that the record in this case showed that 1) the wholly owned subsidiaries of Humana Inc. were insured under the subject policies, 2) the subsidiaries were related to Health Care Indemnity as brother-sister, not as parent-subsidiaries, 3) the amounts due under the subject policies as premiums were billed by Health Care Indemnity to Humana on a monthly basis, 4) Humana paid the total amount billed by Health Care Indemnity on a monthly basis, 5) later, the foregoing amounts were allocated and charged back by Humana, Inc. to its appropriate subsidiaries.

13

The dissent further noted that the majority rested heavily upon the joint opinion of the experts Plotkin and Stewart. However, these opinions gave no support to the position of the majority on the brother-sister question. The thrust of the Plotkin, Stewart testimony was aimed at the parent-subsidiary question, the reasoning being that the subsidiary's stock was shown as an asset on the parent's balance sheet. If the parent suffered an insured loss which a subsidiary had to pay, the assets of the subsidiary insurer would be depleted by the amount of the payment. This, in turn, reduced the value of the subsidiary shares as an asset of the parent. In effect, the assets of the insured parent were bearing the loss as far as the true economic impact was concerned. The dissent claimed that the reasoning presented by the experts provided no support for the majority's position in the brother-sister context. Humana, 88 T.C. at 243-44 (1987) (Korner, J., dissenting). Humana Inc.'s insured subsidiaries owned no stock in Health Care Indemnity, nor vice versa. The subsidiaries' balance sheets and net worth were in no way affected by the payment of an insured claim by Health Care Indemnity. When the subsidiaries paid their own premiums for their own insurance, they shifted their risks to Health Care Indemnity. The dissent argued that the rationale of Carnation and Clougherty thus did not apply. Id. at 247.

14

The dissent further noted that the cases cited by the tax court, Stearns-Roger, Mobil Oil, and Beech Aircraft v. United States, 797 F.2d 920 (10th Cir.1986), each explicitly or implicitly adopted the economic family concept. However, Health Care Indemnity and the hospital subsidiaries were valid separate business entities conducting active legitimate businesses devoid of sham. No facts stated the contrary. The dissent argued that to hold the insurance contracts between them invalid because they are one "economic family" and what happens to one happens to all of them ignored the separate entities of Humana Inc., its hospital subsidiaries, and Health Care Indemnity. Such a holding violated the time honored rule under Moline Properties that each taxpayer is a separate entity for tax purposes.

15

We review de novo the legal standard applied by the tax court in determining whether Humana Inc.'s payments to its captive insurance company, Health Care Indemnity, for itself and on behalf of its subsidiaries constitute ordinary and necessary business expenses for insurance. Rose v. Commissioner, 868 F.2d 851 (6th Cir.1989). The tax court's findings of fact shall not be overturned unless clearly erroneous. Id. at 853.

16

The Internal Revenue Code Sec. 162(a) (1954) allows a deduction for all ordinary and necessary business expenses paid or incurred during the taxable year in carrying on a trade or business. Insurance premiums in the case of a business are generally deductible business expenses. Treas.Reg. Sec. 1.162-1(a) (1954). Although the term "insurance" is not self-defined by the Internal Revenue Code, the Supreme Court in Helvering v. Le Gierse, 312 US 531, 61 S.Ct. 646,

85 L.Ed. 996 (1941), provided the test for defining "insurance" for federal tax purposes.

17

An insurance contract involves (1) risk shifting and (2) risk distribution. Helvering v. Le Gierse, 312 US 531, 539, 61 S.Ct. 646, 649, 85 L.Ed. 996 (1941) (where an annuity contract completely neutralized the risk inherent in a life insurance contract when both contracts were considered together as one transaction). Risk shifting involves the shifting of an identifiable risk of the insured to the insurer. The focus is on the individual contract between the insured and the insurer. Risk distribution involves shifting to a group of individuals the identified risk of the insured. The focus is broader and looks more to the insurer as to whether the risk insured against can be distributed over a larger group rather than the relationship between the insurer and any single insured. Commissioner of Internal Revenue v. Treganowan, 183 F.2d 288, 291 (2nd Cir.), cert. denied, 340 US 853, 71 S.Ct. 82, 95 L.Ed. 625 (1950).

18

We believe that the tax court correctly held on the first issue, the parent-subsidiary issue, that under the principles of Clougherty and Carnation the premiums paid by Humana Inc., the parent to Health Care Indemnity, its wholly owned subsidiary, did not constitute insurance premiums and, therefore, were not deductible. Humana Inc. did not shift the risk to Health Care Indemnity. As the Tenth Circuit stated in Stearns-Roger:

19

The comparison of the arrangement here made to self-insurance cannot be ignored. The parent provided the necessary funds to the subsidiary by way of what it called "premiums" to meet the casualty losses of the parent. The subsidiary retained these funds until paid back to the parent on losses.... In the case before us we must again consider economic reality. The sums were with the subsidiary for future use and would be included in the Stearns-Roger balance sheet. Again the risk of loss did not leave the parent corporation.

20

Stearns-Roger, 774 F.2d at 416-17. We believe the tax court also correctly held that if the subject payments made by the wholly owned subsidiaries were not deductible as insurance premiums, they likewise should be considered additions to a reserve for losses and not deductible under the Internal Revenue Code Sec. 162 (1954) as ordinary and necessary business expenses. Stearns-Roger, 774 F.2d at 415; Mobil Oil, 8 Cl.Ct. at 567; Steere Tank Lines, Inc. v. United States, 577 F.2d 279, 280 (5th Cir.1978), cert. denied 440 US 946, 99 S.Ct. 1424, 59 L.Ed.2d 634 (1979); Spring Canyon Coal v. Commissioner, 43 F.2d 78 (10th Cir.1930), cert. denied 284 US 654, 52 S.Ct. 33, 76 L.Ed. 555 (1931). We find no error in fact or law with regard to this first issue.

21

With regard to the second issue, the brother-sister issue, we believe that the tax court incorrectly extended the rationale of Carnation and Clougherty in holding that the premiums paid by the subsidiaries of Humana Inc. to Health Care Indemnity, as charged to them by Humana Inc., did not constitute valid insurance agreements with the premiums deductible under Internal Revenue Code Sec. 162(a) (1954). We must treat Humana Inc., its subsidiaries and Health Care

Indemnity as separate corporate entities under Moline Properties. When considered as separate entities, the first prong of Le Gierse is clearly met. Risk shifting exists between the subsidiaries and the insurance company. There is simply no direct connection in this case between a loss sustained by the insurance company and the affiliates of Humana Inc. as existed between the parent company and the captive insurance company in both Carnation and Clougherty.

22

In so stating, we adopt the analysis of the Ninth Circuit in Clougherty. It dealt with the parent-subsidiary issue and held that Clougherty could not deduct payments as insurance to Lombardy, its captive insurance company, as there was no risk shifting. Its holding was explained as follows, 811 F.2d at 1305:

23

In reaching our holding, we do not disturb the legal status of the various corporate entities involved, either by treating them as a single unit or otherwise. Rather, we examine the economic consequences of the captive insurance arrangement to the "insured" party to see if that party has, in fact, shifted the risk. In doing so, we look only to the insured's assets, i.e., those of Clougherty.... Viewing only Clougherty's assets and considering only the effect of a claim on those assets, it is clear that the risk of loss has not been shifted from Clougherty. (emphasis added).

24

Because the Ninth Circuit's analysis does "not disturb the separate legal status of the various corporate entities," we adopt the same line of reasoning to decide the brother-sister issue in the case before us. If we look solely to the insured's assets, i.e., those of the various affiliates of Humana Inc., and consider only the effect of a claim on those assets, it is clear that the risk of loss has shifted from the various affiliates to Health Care Indemnity.

25

The only open question is whether there was risk distribution, the second prong of the test for an insurance contract under Le Gierse. We hold that there was both risk shifting and risk distribution between the subsidiaries and the captive insurance company. The tax court, therefore, erred on this second "brother-sister" issue.

26

We recognize, as we must, the separate corporate existence of the affiliates of Humana Inc. and that of Health Care Indemnity. As the Supreme Court stated in Moline Properties, "[S]o long as [its] purpose is the equivalent of business activity or is followed by the carrying on of business by the corporation, the corporation remains a separate taxable entity." Moline Properties, 319 US at 439, 63 S.Ct. at 1134. See Clougherty, 811 F.2d at 1302 (where the Ninth Circuit stated that, "While Moline Properties concerned an attempt by the sole shareholder of a corporation to report on his personal return income attributable to the corporation, the rule it enunciates applies as well to a corporation and its subsidiaries."). See also National Carbide Corporation v. Commissioner, 336 US 422, 429, 69 S.Ct. 726, 730, 93 L.Ed. 779 (1949) (where the Moline Properties doctrine was applied for federal income tax purposes even where a parent corporation controlled its wholly-owned subsidiary). We, therefore, look solely to the relationship between the affiliates and Health Care Indemnity and conclude the facts of this case support a finding of risk shifting as between the affiliates of Humana Inc. and Health Care Indemnity.

27

Health Care Indemnity met the State of Colorado's statutory minimum requirements for an insurance company, was recognized as an insurance company following an audit and certification by the State of Colorado, and is currently a valid insurance company subject to the strict regulatory control of the Colorado Insurance Department. The State of Colorado has either approved or established the premium rate for insurance between the Humana affiliates and Health Care Indemnity. As a valid insurance company under Colorado law, Health Care Indemnity's assets cannot be reached by its shareholders except in conformity with the statute. Colorado Rev. Stat. 10-3-503.

28

Health Care Indemnity was fully capitalized and no agreement ever existed under which the subsidiaries or Humana Inc. would contribute additional capital to Health Care Indemnity. The hospital subsidiaries and Humana Inc. never contributed additional amounts to Health Care Indemnity nor took any steps to insure Health Care Indemnity's performance. It is also undisputed that the policies purchased by the hospital subsidiaries and Humana Inc. were insurance policies as commonly understood in the industry. The hospital subsidiaries and Humana Inc. entered into bona fide arms length contracts with Health Care Indemnity. Health Care Indemnity was formed for legitimate business purposes. Health Care Indemnity and the hospital subsidiaries conduct legitimate businesses and are devoid of sham. No suggestion has been made that the premiums were overstated or understated. Health Care Indemnity did not file its income tax returns on a consolidated basis with Humana Inc. and its subsidiaries. Humana Inc.'s insured subsidiaries own no stock in Health Care Indemnity, nor vice versa.

29

As noted, supra, the tax court majority cites Mobil Oil in support of its holding on the brother-sister issue. The court in Mobil Oil stated that the imposition of a tax must be based on economic reality and the incidence of taxation depends upon the substance of the transaction and the relationship of the parties. Mobil Oil, 8 Cl.Ct. at 567. The economic reality of insurance between a parent and a captive insurance company is that the captive's stock is shown as an asset on the parent's balance sheet. If the parent suffers an insured loss which the captive has to pay, the assets of the captive will be depleted by the amount of the payment. This will reduce the value of the captive's shares as an asset of the parent. In effect, the assets of the parent bear the true economic impact of the loss. The economic reality, however, of insurance between the Humana subsidiaries and Health Care Indemnity, where the subsidiaries own no stock in the captive and vice versa, is that when a loss occurs and is paid by Health Care Indemnity the net worth of the Humana affiliates is not reduced accordingly. The subsidiaries' balance sheets and net worth are not affected by the payment of an insured claim by Health Care Indemnity. In reality, therefore, when the Humana subsidiaries pay their own premiums under their own insurance contracts, as the facts show, they shift their risk to Health Care Indemnity.

30

The tax court majority has argued that Stearns-Roger and Mobil extend the rationale of Carnation and Clougherty to cover the brother-sister factual pattern of Humana in favor of denying deductions of payments by the Humana affiliate corporations. The tax court majority stated that "they likewise extend the rationale to the ... brother-sister factual pattern presented in the case." Humana, 88 T.C. at 217.

31

Neither Carnation nor Clougherty themselves, nor Stearns-Roger nor Mobil Oil provide a basis for denying the deductions in the brother-sister issue. Carnation did not deal with a captive insurance company of a parent corporation insuring separate and distinct wholly owned affiliate corporations of that parent. Carnation dealt solely with the parent-subsidiary issue, not the brother-sister issue. Likewise, Clougherty dealt only with the parent-subsidiary issue and not the brother-sister issue. Nothing in either Carnation or Clougherty lends support for denying the deductibility of the payments in the brother-sister context.

32

Stearns-Roger and Mobil Oil also do not provide a basis for extending Carnation and Clougherty to cover the brother-sister situation because both clearly rest on the economic family argument that the tax court claimed to reject in Humana. The court in Mobil Oil made no distinctions between the various entities involved--Mobil, its domestic and foreign subsidiaries, and the various captive insurance companies. The court treated them all as one economic unit. The court cited for support cases resting on the economic family argument, looked only to the parent and stated that the "risk of loss remains with the parent," and thus there was no insurance. Mobil Oil, 8 Cl.Ct. at 570.

33

The Tenth Circuit in Stearns-Roger v. United States, 774 F.2d 414 (1985), rested its holding impliedly if not expressly on the economic family theory. On appeal pursuant to certification under Sec.

1292(b), the Tenth Circuit affirmed the district court's holding, 577 F.Supp. 833, 838 (1984), in which the district court concluded:

34

Its [Glendale Insurance Company] only business is to insure its parent corporation which wholly owns it and ultimately bears any losses or enjoys any profits it produces. Both profits and losses stay within the Stearns-Roger "economic family." I conclude that since the agreement between Stearns-Roger and Glendale did not shift the risk of losses, it was not an insurance contract for federal tax purposes.[2]

35

The tax court cannot avoid direct confrontation with the separate corporate existence doctrine of Moline Properties by claiming that its decision does not rest on "economic family" principles because it is merely reclassifying or recharacterizing the transaction as nondeductible additions to a reserve for losses. The tax court argues in its opinion that such "recharacterization" does not disregard the separate corporate status of the entities involved, but merely disregards the particular transactions between the entities in order to take into account substance over form and the "economic reality" of the transaction that no risk has shifted.

36

The tax court misapplies this substance over form argument. The substance over form or economic reality argument is not a broad legal doctrine designed to distinguish between legitimate and illegitimate transactions and employed at the discretion of the tax court whenever it feels that a taxpayer is taking advantage of the tax laws to produce a favorable result for the taxpayer. Higgins v. Smith, 308 US 473, 476, 60 S.Ct. 355, 357, 84 L.Ed.406 (1940) (where the

Court stated, "The Government urges that the principle underlying Gregory v. Helvering finds expression in the rule calling for a realistic approach to tax situations. As so broad and unchallenged a principle furnishes only a general direction, it is of little value in the solution of tax problems."). The substance over form analysis, rather, is a distinct and limited exception to the general rule under Moline Properties that separate entities must be respected as such for tax purposes. The substance over form doctrine applies to disregard the separate corporate entity where "Congress has evinced an intent to the contrary...." Clougherty, 811 F.2d at 1302. As the Court stated in Moline, 319 US at 439, 63 S.Ct. at 1134, , "A particular legislative purpose, such as the development of the merchant marine, ... may call for the disregarding of the separate entity, Munson S.S. Line v. Commissioner, 77 F.2d 849 [2nd Cir.1935], as may the necessity of striking down frauds on the tax statute, Continental Oil v. Jones, 113 F.2d 557 [10th Cir.1940]." However, as the Ninth Circuit pointed out in Clougherty, "Congress ... has remained silent with respect to the taxation of captive insurers...." 811 F.2d at 1302. In general, absent specific congressional intent to the contrary, as is the situation in this case, a court cannot disregard a transaction in the name of economic reality and substance over form absent a finding of sham or lack of business purpose under the relevant tax statute. Clougherty, 811 F.2d at 1302; Gregory v. Helvering, 293 US 465, 469, 55 S.Ct. 266, 269, 79 L.Ed. 596 (1935); Higgins v. Smith, 308 US 473, 477, 60 S.Ct. 355, 357, 84 L.Ed. 406 (1940).

37

In the instant case, the tax court found that Humana had a valid business purpose for incorporating Health Care Indemnity. Congress has manifested no intent to disregard the separate corporate entity in the context of captive insurers. In short, the substance over form or economic reality argument under current legal application does not provide any justification for the tax court to reclassify the insurance premiums paid by the subsidiaries of Humana Inc. as nondeductible additions to a reserve for losses. The test to determine whether a transaction under the Internal Revenue Code Sec. 162(a) (1954) is legitimate or illegitimate is not a vague and broad "economic reality" test. The test is whether there is risk shifting and risk distribution. Only if a transaction fails to meet the above two-pronged test can the court justifiably reclassify the transaction as something other than insurance.

38

We have both risk shifting and risk distribution involved in the transactions between the Humana subsidiaries and Health Care Indemnity. The transactions between Health Care Indemnity and the separate affiliates of Humana, therefore, are properly within the statutory language of the Internal Revenue Code Sec. 162(a) (1954) as interpreted in Le Gierse. As long as the transactions meet the purposes of the tax statute, Higgins, 308 US at 477, 60 S.Ct. at 357, the substance of the transactions are valid and legitimate regardless of its form and regardless of the tax motivation on the part of the taxpayers involved, Gregory, 293 US at 469, 55 S.Ct. at 267.

39

We, therefore, find no credence in the distinction between disregarding the particular transactions between the Humana affiliates and Health Care Indemnity and disregarding the separate entities. Absent a fact pattern of sham or lack of business purpose, a court should accept transactions between related though separate corporations as proper and not disregard them because of the relationship between the parties. As the Second Circuit stated in Kraft Foods Company v. Commissioner, 232 F.2d 118, 123-24 (2nd Cir.1956):

40

[I]t is one thing to say that transactions between affiliates should be carefully scrutinized and sham transactions disregarded, and quite a different thing to say that a genuine transaction affecting legal relations should be disregarded for tax purposes merely because it is a transaction between affiliated corporations. We think that to strike down a genuine transaction because of a parent's subsidiary relation would violate the scheme of the statute and depart from the rules of law heretofore governing inter-company transactions.

41

Id. 123-24.

42

Finally, the tax court argues that if it did not deny the deductions in the brother-sister context, Humana Inc. could avoid the tax court's holding on issue one, the parent-captive issue, that insurance premiums paid by the parent to a captive insurance company are not deductible and accomplish the same purpose through its subsidiaries. Such an argument provides no legal justification for denying the deduction in the brother-sister context. The legal test is whether there has been risk distribution and risk shifting, not whether Humana Inc. is a common parent or whether its affiliates are in a brother-sister relationship to Health Care Indemnity. We do not focus on the relationship of the parties per se or the particular structure of the corporation involved. We look to the assets of the insured. Clougherty, 811 F.2d at 1305. If Humana changes its corporate structure and that change involves risk shifting and risk distribution, and that change is for a legitimate business purpose and is not a sham to avoid the payment of taxes, then it is irrelevant whether the changed corporate structure has the side effect of also permitting Humana Inc.'s affiliates to take advantage of the Internal Revenue Code Sec. 162(a) (1954) and deduct payments to a captive insurance company under the control of the Humana parent as insurance premiums.

43

The Commissioner argues for us to adopt its economic family approach because this approach recognizes the economic reality of the transaction between Humana affiliates and the captive insurance company, Health Care Indemnity. We do not, however, as the government argues, look to Humana Inc., the parent, to determine whether premiums paid by the affiliates to Health Care Indemnity are deductible. To do so would be to treat Humana Inc., its affiliates and Health Care Indemnity as one "economic unit" and ignore the reality of their separate corporate existence for tax purposes in violation of Moline Properties. Even the tax court explicitly rejected the Commissioner's economic family argument. Humana, 88 T.C. at 230.[3]

44

The Commissioner has also argued that even if we do not adopt the economic family argument, we should look through the form of the transaction between the Humana affiliates and Health Care Indemnity to the substance of the transaction and hold that in substance there was no risk shifting. It would appear that this is just another way of stating that transactions between affiliates for tax purposes shall be disregarded if devoid of business purposes or a sham. We have already discussed in detail this exception to Moline Properties, supra. However, if the Commissioner's form over substance or "economic reality" argument is an attempt to broaden the "sham" exception or fashion a new exception, we reject the argument.

45

Treating the Humana affiliates and Health Care Indemnity as separate entities and rejecting the economic family argument leads to the conclusion that the first prong of the Le Gierse test for determining "insurance" has been met--there is risk shifting between the Humana affiliates and Health Care Indemnity. However, we must also satisfy the second prong of Le Gierse and find risk distribution. As stated, supra, risk distribution involves shifting to a group of individuals the identified risk of the insured. The focus is broader and looks more to the insurer as to whether the risk insured against can be distributed over a larger group rather than the relationship between the insurer and any single insured. Commissioner of Internal Revenue v. Treganowan, 183 F.2d 288, 291 (2nd Cir.), cert. denied, 340 US 853, 71 S.Ct. 82, 95 L.Ed. 625 (1950). There is little authority adequately discussing what constitutes risk distribution if there is risk shifting. Just recently, the tax court in Gulf Oil v. Commissioner, 89 T.C. 1010, 1035 (1987), noted that insurance must consist of both risk shifting and risk distribution and that the definition of an insurance contract depended on meeting both of the prongs.[4] With this we firmly agree. Risk transfer and risk distribution are two separate and distinct prongs of the test and both must be met to create an insurance contract. An arrangement between a parent corporation and a captive insurance company in which the captive insures only the risks of the parent might not result in risk distribution. Any loss by the parent is not subject to the premiums of any other entity. However, we see no reason why there would not be risk distribution in the instant case where the captive insures several separate corporations within an affiliated group and losses can be spread among the several distinct corporate entities.

46

In conclusion, we affirm the tax court on issue one, the parent-subsidiary issue. The contracts between Humana, Inc., the parent, and Health Care Indemnity, the wholly owned captive insurance company, are not insurance contracts and the premiums are not deductible under the Internal Revenue Code Sec. 162(a) (1954). We reverse the tax court on issue two, the brother-sister issue. The contracts between the affiliates of Humana Inc. and Health Care Indemnity are in substance insurance contracts and the premiums are deductible. Under Moline Properties, we must recognize the affiliates as separate and distinct corporations from Humana Inc., the parent company, and, as such, they shifted their risk to Health Care Indemnity. Furthermore, we find there was risk distribution on the part of Health Care Indemnity given the number of separate though related corporations insured by Health Care Indemnity. Under no circumstances do we adopt the economic family argument advanced by the government.

47

Thus the Tax Court is affirmed on Issue One, Reversed on Issue Two and the case remanded for recomputation of the tax due.

[Footnote] 1

Humana Incorporated owns 75 percent of Health Care Indemnity and Humana's Netherlands affiliate owns 25 percent. Technically, therefore, Humana is not a 100 percent owner of Health Care Indemnity. However, the tax court stated, and both parties agreed, that the only business purpose of the offshore affiliate was to provide capital for Health Care Indemnity. Therefore, the court and both parties agreed to treat Health Care Indemnity as a wholly-owned subsidiary of Humana.

[Footnote] 2

The Carnation case involved an undercapitalized foreign captive, with a capitalization agreement running to the captive from the parent. Stearns-Roger, although involving an adequately capitalized domestic captive, involved an indemnification agreement running from the parent to the captive. A third case, Beech Aircraft, 797 F.2d 920 (10th Cir. 1986), mentioned as support for the majority position, also involved an undercapitalized captive. These weaknesses alone provided a sufficient basis from which to find no risk shifting and to decide the cases in favor of the Commissioner. The Humana case contained no such indemnification agreement and Health Care Indemnity was adequately capitalized.

[Footnote] 3

Although the tax court in the present case disclaims reliance on the economic family theory, its holding appears ultimately premised on the same type of analysis. In effect the tax court holds that one corporate entity cannot shift risk of loss in an insurance transaction to another corporate entity if they are in the same affiliated group. This approach conflicts with the Moline Properties rule of separate corporate entities. As the eight member concurrence written by Judge Whitaker pointed out:

> However, the majority refers repeatedly with apparent approval to decisions of other courts, including the opinion of the Court of Appeals of the Ninth Circuit affirming our opinion in Carnation, all of which follow Carnation and

> adopt the economic family concept. The majority also quotes extensively with approval from the testimony of respondent's experts, Dr. Plotkin and Mr. Stewart, who have fully swallowed respondent's economic family concept.... For these reasons, I strongly believe that we should decide the issue solely on a lack of risk shifting and risk distribution basis.

Humana, 88 T.C. 197, 231 (1987) (Whitaker, J., concurring).

It is this argument that we consider more logically sound than the majority. We disagree, however, in the application of the argument and find the existence of risk shifting and risk distribution.

[Footnote] 4

The tax court noted in Gulf Oil, decided shortly after this Humana case, that if a captive insurance company insured unrelated interests outside the affiliated group of the captive insurance company, then there might be adequate risk transfer created by insuring the risks of independent third parties. The majority held that the addition of 2 percent of unrelated premiums is de minimis and would not satisfy the majority that the risk was transferred. However, if the premium income from unrelated parties was at least 50 percent, the majority stated that there would be sufficient risk transfer so that the arrangement would constitute insurance and premiums paid by the parent and affiliates to the captive insurance company would be deductible under the Internal Revenue Code Sec. 162(a) (1954). It is unclear in the language employed by the tax court majority in Gulf Oil whether the appearance of unrelated third-party premiums constitutes risk shifting or risk distribution. The tax court majority refers to the appearance of unrelated third-parties as sufficient to constitute "risk transfer." If the appearance of unrelated third-parties creates "risk transfer" and by this the tax court means both risk shifting and risk distribution, the tax court majority ignores the fact that risk shifting and risk distribution are two separate and distinct prongs. The tax court majority cannot collapse the two prong test into one and claim that the appearance of unrelated third-parties creates enough risk transfer. Such is not the law. If the presence of unrelated third-parties goes to the question of risk distribution, then the tax court majority should never have reached that issue as its prior opinions, especially its opinion in Humana, stated that there can be no risk shifting as between a captive insurance company and a parent and its affiliated corporations where both are owned by a common parent, as was the situation in Gulf Oil. Thus the tax court has created its own conflict between its holding in Humana and its holding in Gulf Oil.

3. Harper Group v. Commissioner, 979 F.2d 1341 (9th Cir. 1992): 979 F.2d 1341

The Harper Group, and Includible Subsidiaries, Petitioners-appellees, v. Commissioner of Internal Revenue Service, Respondent-appellant

United States Court of Appeals, Ninth Circuit—979 F.2d 1341

Argued and Submitted Oct. 9, 1992. Decided Nov. 5, 1992.

John A. Dudeck, Jr., and Gary R. Allen, US Dept. of Justice, Tax Div., Appellate Section, Washington, D.C., for respondent-appellant.

Paul J. Sax and William L. Riley, Orrick, Herrington & Sutcliffe, San Francisco, Cal., for petitioner-appellee.

Appeal from a Decision of the United States Tax Court.

Before: POOLE, FERNANDEZ, and T.G. NELSON, Circuit Judges.

FERNANDEZ, Circuit Judge:

1

The Harper Group (Harper) and certain of its domestic subsidiaries purchased insurance policies from Rampart Insurance Co. Ltd. (Rampart) and deducted the premiums for income tax purposes. Rampart is a wholly owned subsidiary of two of Harper's subsidiaries. The Commissioner of Internal Revenue (Commissioner) determined that because of the relationship among the parties the transactions did not constitute insurance. A notice of deficiency was issued by the Commissioner, and Harper and its subsidiaries petitioned the Tax Court for a redetermination. The Tax Court found that the transactions were insurance.[1] It, therefore, held against the Commissioner who now appeals. We affirm.

2

In AMERCO, Inc. v. Commissioner, 979 F.2d 162 (9th Cir.1992) we decided that it is possible to have a true insurance transaction between a corporation and its wholly owned insurance company if that captive does substantial unrelated insurance business. Likewise other members of the corporate group can have true insurance transactions with the captive. The result is that insurance premiums paid by the parent or the other members of the group are deductible by them. The only relevant way in which this case differs from AMERCO is that here the unrelated business of the captive was from 29 percent to 33 percent of its total business, rather than the 52 percent to 74 percent found in AMERCO.

3

Prior cases which have found true insurance have also included higher percentages of unrelated business than those found here. See Sears Roebuck & Co. v. Commissioner, 972 F.2d 858, 860 (7th Cir.1992) (99.75 percent from others); Ocean Drilling & Exploration Co. v. United States, 24 Cl.Ct. 714, 730 (1991) (44 percent to 66 percent from others).

4

Cases which have found no true insurance have found much lower percentages of unrelated business. See, e.g., Beech Aircraft Corp. v. United States, 797 F.2d 920, 921-22 (10th Cir.1986) (.5 percent from others); Gulf Oil Corp. v. Commissioner, 89 T.C. 1010, 1028 (1987) (2 percent from others), rev'd in part on other grounds, 914 F.2d 396 (3d Cir.1990); Clougherty Packing Co. v. Commissioner, 811 F.2d 1297, 1299 (9th Cir.1987) (none from others).

5

Thus, it is undoubtedly true that the existence of insurance is obvious in some cases. Moreover, there is a point at which the amount of outside business is insubstantial, so true insurance does not exist.

6

The Tax Court found that the point of insubstantiality had not been reached in this case. We cannot say that it committed clear error in so deciding.

7

AFFIRMED.

[Footnote] 1

Harper Group and Includible Subsidiaries v. Commissioner, 96 T.C. 45 (1991).

4. Revenue Ruling 77-316:

REVENUE RULING 77-316, 1977-2 C.B. 53, amplified in Rev. Rul. 88-72, declared obsolete in Rev. Rul. 2001-31.

Wholly owned foreign "insurance" subsidiary. Examples illustrate the tax consequences of so-called insurance premiums paid by a domestic corporation and its domestic subsidiaries to the parent's wholly owned foreign "insurance" subsidiary and compensation received from the foreign "insurance" subsidiary with respect to "insured" losses incurred by the domestic parent and subsidiaries.

Rev. Rul. 77-316

Advice has been requested whether, under each of the three situations described below, amounts paid as insurance premiums by a domestic parent corporation and its domestic subsidiaries to a wholly owned foreign "insurance" subsidiary of the parent are deductible as ordinary and necessary business expenses under section 162 of the Internal Revenue Code of 1954. Advice has also been requested whether deductions for losses that are incurred by the domestic parent and its domestic subsidiaries and that are otherwise allowable under section 165(a), will be reduced by amounts received from the "insurance" subsidiary with respect to risks retained by the "insurance" subsidiary. In addition, advice has been requested whether the wholly owned foreign "insurance" subsidiary in each situation described below qualifies as an insurance company for Federal income tax purposes.

Situation 1 During the taxable year domestic corporation *X* and its domestic subsidiaries entered into a contract for fire and other casualty insurance with *S1,* a newly organized wholly owned foreign "insurance" subsidiary of *X*. *S1* was organized to insure properties and other casualty risks of *X* and its domestic subsidiaries. *X* and its domestic subsidiaries paid amounts as casualty insurance premiums directly to *S1*. Such amounts reflect commercial rates for the insurance involved. *S1* has not accepted risks from parties other than *X* and its domestic subsidiaries.

Situation 2 The facts are the same as set forth in *Situation 1* except that domestic corporation *Y* and its domestic subsidiaries paid amounts as casualty insurance premiums to *M*, an unrelated domestic insurance company. This insurance was placed with *M* under a contractual arrangement that provided that *M* would immediately transfer 95 percent of the risks under reinsurance agreements to *S2*, the wholly owned foreign "insurance" subsidiary of *Y*. However, the contractual arrangement for reinsurance did not relieve *M* of its liability as the primary insurer of *Y* and its domestic subsidiaries; nor was there any collateral agreement between *M* and *Y*, or any of *Y*'s subsidiaries, to reimburse *M* in the event that *S2* could not meet its reinsurance obligations.

Situation 3 The facts are the same as set forth in *Situation 1* except that domestic corporation *Z* and its domestic subsidiaries paid amounts as casualty insurance premiums directly to *Z*'s wholly-owned foreign "insurance" subsidiary, *S3*. Contemporaneous with the acceptance of this insurance risk, and pursuant to a contractual obligation to *Z* and its domestic subsidiaries, *S3* transferred 90 percent of the risk through reinsurance agreements to an unrelated insurance company, *W*.

Section 162(a) of the Code provides, in part, that there shall be allowed as a deduction all the ordinary and necessary expenses paid or incurred during the taxable year in carrying on any trade or business.

Section 1.162-1(a) of the Income Tax Regulations provides, in part, that among the items included in business expenses are insurance premiums against fire, storms, theft, accident, or other similar losses in the case of a business.

Historically, insurance involves risk-shifting and risk-distributing, and the sharing and distribution of the insurance risk by all the parties insured is essential to the concept of true insurance. See Helvering v. Le Gierse, 312 US 531 (1941); Commissioner v. Treganowan, 183 F. 2d 188 (2d Cir. 1950); and Rev. Rul. 60-275, 1960-2 C.B. 43. Thus, when there is no economic shift or distribution of the risk "insured," the contract is not one of insurance, and the premiums therefor are not deductible under section 1.162-1(a) of the regulations.

Also, both the Internal Revenue Service and the courts have long held that amounts set aside by a taxpayer as a reserve for self-insurance, though equal to commercial insurance premiums, are not deductible for Federal income tax purposes as "ordinary and necessary expenses paid or incurred during the taxable year." See Rev. Rul. 60-275, Rev. Rul. 57-485, 1957-2 C.B. 117, and Pan American Hide Co. v. Commissioner, 1 B.T.A. 1249 (1925). Even where a self-insurance fund is administered by an independent agent, such fact does not make payments to such fund deductible. See Spring Canyon Coal Company v. [Commissioner], 43 F.2d 78 (10th Cir. 1930), cert. denied, 284 US 654 (1930).

Under the three situations described, there is no economic shifting or distributing of risks of loss with respect to the risks carried or retained by the wholly owned foreign subsidiaries, *S1, S2,* and *S3,* respectively. In each situation described, the insuring parent corporation and its domestic subsidiaries, and the wholly owned "insurance" subsidiary, though separate corporate entities, represent one economic family with the result that those who bear the ultimate economic burden of loss are the same persons who suffer the loss. To the extent that the risks of loss are not retained in their entirety by (as in *Situation 2*) or reinsured with (as in *Situation 3*) insurance companies that are unrelated to the economic family of insureds, there is no risk-shifting or risk-distributing, and no insurance, the premiums for which are deductible under section 162 of the Code.

Thus, the amounts paid by *X, Y,* and *Z,* and their domestic subsidiaries, and retained by *S1* (100 percent), *S2* (95 percent), and *S3* (10 percent), respectively, are not deductible under section 162 of the Code as "ordinary and necessary expenses paid or incurred during the taxable year." Because such amounts remain within the economic family and under the practical control of the respective parent in each situation, there has been no amount "paid or incurred." See Rev. Rul. 60-275, and Rev. Rul. 69-512, 1969-2 C.B. 24.

However, in *Situation 2,* to the extent the unrelated insurer, *M,* retains the risks (5 percent) that are not reinsured by *S2,* and in *Situation 3,* to the extent *S3* transfers the risks (90 percent) through reinsurance agreements to *W,* the unrelated reinsurer, that portion of the premiums paid by *Y* and *Z* and their domestic subsidiaries to cover these risks are deductible under section 162 of the Code. Since these amounts are not withdrawable by either *Y* and its domestic subsidiaries or *Z* and its domestic subsidiaries, they have been "paid or incurred" within the meaning of section 162. Furthermore, the requisite shifting and distribution of the risks has occurred to the extent the unrelated insurers, *M* and *W,* respectively, bear the risks of loss.

Amounts paid as so-called insurance premiums by *X, Y,* and *Z,* and their domestic subsidiaries, with respect to risks remaining with *S1,*

S2, and *S3,* respectively, will not constitute taxable income to *S1, S2,* and *S3* under section 61 of the Code as nothing has occurred other than a movement of an asset (cash) within each family of related corporations. Instead such amounts will be considered contributions of capital under section 118.

Because the parent through its control of the corporate family members (its domestic subsidiaries and its wholly owned foreign subsidiary) has control over the movement of assets within the family, the payments of so-called "insurance" premiums made by the domestic subsidiaries of *X, Y,* and *Z* to *S1, S2,* and *S3,* respectively, to the extent of available earnings and profits, are viewed first as a distribution of dividends under section 301 of the Code from such subsidiaries (equal to premiums paid that end up in the foreign "insurance" subsidiary) to their respective parents and then as a contribution of capital by the parents to the respective foreign subsidiaries. Compare Rev. Rul. 69-630, 1969-2 C.B. 112, discussing the treatment of a "bargain sale" between two corporate entities controlled by the same shareholders.

Furthermore, any proceeds paid by *S1, S2,* and *S3* to their respective parents or the parents' domestic subsidiaries with respect to risks of loss retained by *S1, S2,* and *S3* are viewed, to the extent of available earnings and profits, as distributions under section 301 of the Code to the respective parent. Specifically, proceeds paid by *S1, S2,* and *S3* to domestic subsidiaries of their respective parents are viewed, to the extent of available earnings and profits, as distributions under section 301 to the respective parent followed by a contribution of capital from the respective parent to the domestic subsidiary.

The preceding analysis recognizes *S1, S2,* and *S3* as independent corporate entities in view of their business activities (Moline Properties v. Commissioner, 319 US 436 (1943), 1943 C.B. 1011), but also examines the economic reality of each situation described. It is concluded that the "insurance agreement" with respect to the risks retained by *S1, S2,* and *S3* is designed to obtain a deduction by indirect means that would be denied if sought directly.

The second issue relates to whether any loss otherwise allowable to *X, Y,* and *Z* and their respective domestic subsidiaries under section 165 of the Code would be reduced by the proceeds received from *S1, S2,* and *S3* to the extent such payments are with respect to risks retained by *S1, S2,* and *S3*. Section 165(a) provides as a general rule that there shall be allowed as a deduction any loss sustained during the taxable year and not compensated for by insurance or otherwise.

Consistent with the reasons given above in denying the deduction of the amounts paid as insurance premiums by *X, Y,* and *Z* and their respective domestic subsidiaries, any benefits paid by *S1, S2,* and *S3* to their respective parents and affiliates could not qualify as compensation by insurance or otherwise to the extent they result from the risks remaining with *S1, S2,* and *S3*. Accordingly, *X* and its domestic subsidiaries in *Situation 1* are entitled to a deduction under section 165(a) of the Code for any losses sustained during the taxable year, since the losses are not compensated by insurance or otherwise. *Y* and its domestic subsidiaries in *Situation 2* are entitled to a deduction for losses sustained during the taxable year to the extent not compensated for by insurance (that is, not compensated by insurance relating to risks assumed by *M*). *Z* and its domestic subsidiaries in *Situation 3* are entitled to a deduction for losses sustained during the taxable year to the extent not compensated for by insurance (that is, not compensated by insurance relating to risks reinsured by *W*).

The final issue is whether *S1, S2,* or *S3* qualifies as an insurance company for Federal income tax purposes. Section 1.831-3(a) of the regulations (applicable generally to stock casualty insurance companies) provides, in part, that the term "insurance companies" means only those companies that qualify as insurance companies under the definition provided by section 1.801-1(b), predecessor to section 1.801-3(a).

Section 1.801-3(a) of the regulations defines an insurance company for purposes of subchapter L as follows:

> The term "insurance company" means a company whose primary and predominant business activity during the taxable year is the issuing of insurance or annuity contracts or the reinsuring of risks underwritten by insurance companies. Thus, though its name, charter powers, and subjection to State insurance laws are significant in determining the business which a company is authorized and intends to carry on, it is the character of the business actually done in the taxable year which determines whether a company is taxable as an insurance company under the Internal Revenue Code.

The question, therefore, is whether *S1, S2,* and *S3* are primarily and predominantly engaged in the insurance business, either by virtue of their assuming a portion of the risks of their respective parents and the parents' domestic subsidiaries, or on the basis of the business it transfers for reinsurance with unrelated insurance companies. Since the arrangement whereby *S1, S2,* and *S3* assume a portion of the risks of their respective corporate families is not insurance under the standards set forth in Le Gierse, such an arrangement does not constitute the issuing of insurance or annuity contracts or the reinsuring of risks underwritten by insurance companies as stated in section

1.801-3(a)(1) of the regulations. Also, *S3* is not engaged in the business of insurance by transferring the risks of its parent corporation and affiliates to an unrelated insurance company because, under a reinsurance agreement, there will be no shifting to or assumption by *S3* of any risk constituting insurance. See Rev. Rul. 56-106, 1956-1 C.B. 313, for the proposition that an insurance company that disposes of its insurance business under a reinsurance agreement ceases to be an insurance company on the effective date of the agreement and thereafter becomes taxable as an ordinary corporation.

Accordingly, *S1, S2,* and *S3,* as described above, are not insurance companies within the definition of section 1.801-3(a)(1) of the regulations because their primary and predominant business activity is not the issuing of insurance and annuity contracts or the reinsuring of risks underwritten by other insurance companies.

5. Revenue Ruling 2001-31:

Section 118.—Contributions to the Capital of a Corporation

26 CFR 1.118–1: Contributions to the capital of a corporation.

The revenue ruling obsoletes Rev. Rul. 77–316 (1977–2 C.B. 53), which provided that payments between related parties that were disallowed as deductions for insurance premiums should be recharacterized as contributions to capital under I.R.C. § 118. See Rev. Rul. 2001–31, on this page.

Section 162.—Trade or Business Expenses

26 CFR 1.162–1: Business expenses.

The revenue ruling announces that the Service will not raise the economic family theory, originally set forth in Rev. Rul. 77–316 (1977–2 C.B. 53), in determining whether payments between related parties are deductible insurance premiums. See Rev. Rul. 2001–31, on this page.

26 CFR 1.162–1: Business expenses. (Also §§ 118, 165, 301, 801, 831; 1.118–1, 1.165–1, 1.301–1, 1.801–3, 1.831–3.)

This ruling explains that the Service will no longer raise the "economic family theory" set forth in Rev. Rul. 77–316 (1977–2 C.B. 53), in addressing whether captive insurance transactions constitute valid insurance. Rather, the Service will address captive insurance transactions on a case-by-case basis.

Rev. Rul. 2001–31

In Rev. Rul. 77–316 (1977–2 C.B. 53), three situations were presented in which a taxpayer attempted to seek insurance coverage for itself and its operating subsidiaries through the taxpayer's wholly-owned captive insurance subsidiary. The ruling explained that the taxpayer, its non-insurance subsidiaries, and its captive insurance subsidiary represented one "economic family" for purposes of analyzing whether transactions involved sufficient risk shifting and risk distribution to constitute insurance for federal income tax purposes. See Helvering v. Le Gierse, 312 US 531 (1941). The ruling concluded that the transactions were not insurance to the extent that risk was retained within that economic family. Therefore, the premiums paid by the taxpayer and its non-insurance subsidiaries to the captive insurer were not deductible.

No court, in addressing a captive insurance transaction, has fully accepted the economic family theory set forth in Rev. Rul. 77–316. See, e.g., Humana, Inc. v. Commissioner, 881 F.2d 247 (6th Cir. 1989); Clougherty Packing Co. v. Commissioner, 811 F.2d 1297 (9th Cir. 1987) (employing a balance sheet test, rather than the economic family theory, to conclude that transaction between parent and subsidiary was not insurance); Kidde Industries, Inc. v. United States, 40 Fed. Cl. 42 (1997). Accordingly, the Internal Revenue Service will no longer invoke the economic family theory with respect to captive insurance transactions.

The Service may, however, continue to challenge certain captive insurance transactions based on the facts and circumstances of each case. See, e.g., Malone & Hyde v. Commissioner, 62 F.3d 835 (6th Cir. 1995) (concluding that brother-sister transactions were not insurance because the taxpayer guaranteed the captive's performance and the captive was thinly capitalized and loosely regulated); Clougherty Packing Co. v. Commissioner (concluding that a transaction between parent and subsidiary was not insurance).

EFFECT ON OTHER DOCUMENTS

Rev. Rul. 77–316, 1977–2 C.B. 53; Rev. Rul. 78–277, 1978–2 C.B. 268; Rev. Rul. 88–72, 1988–2 C.B. 31; and Rev. Rul. 89–61, 1989–1 C.B. 75, are obsoleted.

Rev. Rul. 78–338, 1978–2 C.B. 107; Rev. Rul. 80–120, 1980–1 C.B. 41; Rev. Rul. 92–93, 1992–2 C.B. 45; and Rev. Proc. 2000–3, 2000–1 I.R.B. 103, are modified.

* * *

6. Revenue Ruling 2002-89:

Section 162.—Trade or Business Expenses

26 CFR 1.162–1: Business expenses. (Also §§ 801, 831.)

Captive insurance. This ruling considers circumstances under which arrangements between a domestic parent corporation and its wholly owned insurance subsidiary constitute insurance for federal income tax purposes.

Rev. Rul. 2002–89

ISSUE

Are the amounts paid by a domestic parent corporation to its wholly owned insurance subsidiary deductible as "insurance premiums" under § 162 of the Internal Revenue Code?

FACTS

Situation 1. P, a domestic corporation, enters into an annual arrangement with its wholly owned domestic subsidiary *S* whereby *S* "insures" the professional liability risks of *P* either directly or as a reinsurer of these risks. *S* is regulated as an insurance company in each state where *S* does business.

The amounts *P* pays to *S* under the arrangement are established according to customary industry rating formulas. In all respects, the parties conduct themselves consistently with the standards applicable to an insurance arrangement between unrelated parties.

In implementing the arrangement, *S* may perform all necessary administrative tasks, or it may outsource those tasks at prevailing commercial market rates. *P* does not provide any guarantee of *S's* performance, and all funds and business records of *P* and *S* are separately maintained. *S* does not loan any funds to *P*.

In addition to the arrangement with *P*, *S* enters into insurance contracts whereby *S* serves as a direct insurer or a reinsurer of the professional liability risks of entities unrelated to *P* or *S*. The risks of unrelated entities and those of *P* are homogeneous. The amounts *S* receives from these unrelated entities under these insurance contracts likewise are established according to customary industry rating formulas.

The premiums *S* earns from the arrangement with *P* constitute 90 percent of *S's* total premiums earned during the taxable year on both a gross and net basis. The liability coverage *S* provides to *P* accounts for 90 percent of the total risks borne by *S*.

Situation 2. Situation 2 is the same as Situation 1 except that the premiums *S* earns from the arrangement with *P* constitute less than 50 percent of *S's* total premiums earned during the taxable year on both a gross and net basis. The liability coverage *S* provides to *P* accounts for less that 50 percent of the total risks borne by *S*.

LAW AND ANALYSIS

Section 162(a) of the Code provides, in part, that there shall be allowed as a deduction all the ordinary and necessary expenses paid or incurred during the taxable year in carrying on any trade or business.

Section 1.162–1(a) of the Income Tax Regulations provides, in part, that among the items included in business expenses are insurance premiums against fire, storms, theft, accident, or other similar losses in the case of a business.

Neither the Code nor the regulations define the terms "insurance" or "insurance contract." The United States Supreme Court, however, has explained that in order for an arrangement to constitute insurance for federal income tax purposes, both risk shifting and risk distribution must be present. Helvering v. LeGierse, 312 US 531 (1941).

Risk shifting occurs if a person facing the possibility of an economic loss transfers some or all of the financial consequences of the potential loss to the insurer, such that a loss by the insured does not affect the insured because the loss is offset by the insurance payment. Risk distribution incorporates the statistical phenomenon known as the law of large numbers. Distributing risk allows the insurer to reduce the possibility that a single costly claim will exceed the amount taken in as premiums and set aside for the payment of such a claim. By assuming numerous relatively small, independent risks that occur randomly over time, the insurer smooths out losses to match more closely its receipt of premiums. Clougherty Packing Co. v. Commissioner, 811 F.2d 1297, 1300 (9th Cir. 1987). Risk distribution necessarily entails a pooling of premiums, so that a potential insured is not in significant part paying for its own risks. See Humana, Inc. v. Commissioner, 881 F.2d 247, 257 (6th Cir. 1989).

No court has held that a transaction between a parent and its wholly-owned subsidiary satisfies the requirements of risk shifting and risk distribution if only the risks of the parent are "insured." See Stearns-Roger Corp. v. United States, 774 F.2d 414 (10th Cir. 1985); Carnation Co. v. Commissioner, 640 F.2d 1010 (9th Cir. 1981), cert. denied 454 US 965 (1981). However, courts have held that an arrangement between a parent and its subsidiary can constitute insurance because the parent's premiums are pooled with those of unrelated parties if (i) insurance risk is present, (ii) risk is shifted and distributed, and (iii) the transaction is of the type that is insurance in the commonly accepted sense. See, e.g., Ocean Drilling & Exploration Co. v. United States, 988 F.2d 1135 (Fed. Cir. 1993); AMERCO, Inc. v. Commissioner, 979 F.2d 162 (9th Cir. 1992).

S is regulated as an insurance company in each state in which it transacts business, and the arrangements between *P* and *S* and between *S* and entities unrelated to *P* or *S* are established and conducted consistently with the standards applicable to an insurance arrangement. *P* does not guarantee *S's* performance and *S* does not make any loans to *P*; *P's* and *S's* funds and records are separately maintained. The narrow question presented in *Situation 1* and *Situation 2* is whether *S* underwrites sufficient risks of unrelated parties that the arrangement between *P* and *S* constitutes insurance for federal income tax purposes.

In *Situation 1,* the premiums that *S* earns from its arrangement with *P* constitute 90 percent of its total premiums earned during the taxable year on both a gross and a net basis. The liability coverage *S* provides to *P* accounts for 90 percent of the total risks borne by *S*. No court has treated such an arrangement between a parent and its wholly-owned subsidiary as insurance. To the contrary, the arrangement lacks the requisite risk shifting and risk distribution to constitute insurance for federal income tax purposes.

In *Situation 2,* the premiums that *S* earns from its arrangement with *P* constitute less than 50 percent of the total premiums *S* earned during the taxable year on both a gross and a net basis. The liability coverage *S* provides to *P* accounts for less than 50 percent of the total risks borne by *S*. The premiums and risks of *P* are thus pooled with those of the unrelated insureds. The requisite risk shifting and risk distribution to constitute insurance for federal income tax purposes are present. The arrangement is insurance in the commonly accepted sense.

HOLDINGS

In *Situation 1,* the arrangement between *P* and *S* does not constitute insurance for federal income tax purposes, and amounts paid by *P* to *S* pursuant to that arrangement are not deductible as "insurance premiums" under § 162.

In *Situation 2,* the arrangement between *P* and *S* constitutes insurance for federal income tax purposes, and the amounts paid by *P* to *S* pursuant to that arrangement are deductible as "insurance premiums" under § 162.

EFFECT ON OTHER DOCUMENTS

Rev. Rul. 2001–31, 2001–1 C.B. 1348, is amplified.

* * *

7. Revenue Ruling 2002-90:

[IRS Synopsis] Captive insurance. This ruling considers circumstances under which payments for professional liability coverage by a number of operating subsidiaries to an insurance subsidiary of a common parent constitute insurance for federal income tax purposes.

Rev. Rul. 2002–90

ISSUE

Are the amounts paid for professional liability coverage by domestic operating subsidiaries to an insurance subsidiary of a common parent deductible as "insurance premiums" under § 162 of the Internal Revenue Code?

FACTS

P, a domestic holding company, owns all of the stock of 12 domestic subsidiaries that provide professional services. Each subsidiary in the *P* group has a geographic territory comprised of a state in which the subsidiary provides professional services. The subsidiaries in the *P* group operate on a decentralized basis. The services provided by the employees of each subsidiary are performed under the general guidance of a supervisory professional for a particular facility of the subsidiary. The general categories of the professional services rendered by each of the subsidiaries are the same throughout the *P* group. Together the 12 subsidiaries have a significant volume of independent, homogeneous risks.

P, for a valid non-tax business purpose, forms *S* as a wholly-owned insurance subsidiary under the laws of State C. *P* provides *S* adequate capital and *S* is fully licensed in State *C* and in the 11 other states where the respective operating subsidiaries conduct their professional service businesses. *S* directly insures the professional liability risks of the 12 operating subsidiaries in the *P* group. *S* charges the 12 subsidiaries arms-length premiums, which are established according to customary industry rating formulas. None of the operating subsidiaries have liability coverage for less than 5 percent, nor more than 15 percent, of the total risk insured by *S*. *S* retains the risks that it insures from the 12 operating subsidiaries. There are no parental (or other related party) guarantees of any kind made in favor of *S*. *S* does not loan any funds to *P* or to the 12 operating subsidiaries. In all respects, the parties conduct themselves in a manner consistent with the standards applicable to an insurance arrangement between unrelated parties. *S* does not provide coverage to any entity other than the 12 operating subsidiaries.

LAW AND ANALYSIS

Section 162(a) of the Code provides, in part, that there shall be allowed as a deduction all the ordinary and necessary expenses paid or incurred during the taxable year in carrying on any trade or business.

Section 1.162–1(a) of the Income Tax Regulations provides, in part, that among the items included in business expenses are insurance premiums against fire, storms, theft, accident, or other similar losses in the case of a business.

Neither the Code nor the regulations define the terms "insurance" or "insurance contract." The United States Supreme Court, however, has explained that in order for an arrangement to constitute "insurance" for federal income tax purposes, both risk shifting and risk distribution must be present. Helvering v. LeGierse, 312 US 531 (1941).

Risk shifting occurs if a person facing the possibility of an economic loss transfers some or all of the financial consequences of the potential loss to the insurer, such that a loss by the insured does not affect the insured because the loss is offset by the insurance payment. Risk distribution incorporates the statistical phenomenon known as the law of large numbers. Distributing risk allows the insurer to reduce the possibility that a single costly claim will exceed the amount taken in as premiums and set aside for the payment of such a claim. By assuming numerous relatively small, independent risks that occur randomly over time, the insurer smooths out losses to match more closely its receipt of premiums. Clougherty Packing Co. v. Commissioner, 811 F.2d 1297, 1300 (9th Cir. 1987). Risk distribution necessarily entails a pooling of premiums, so that a potential insured is not in significant part paying for its own risks. See Humana Inc. v. Commissioner, 881 F.2d 247, 257 (6th Cir. 1989).

In Humana, the United States Court of Appeals for the Sixth Circuit held that arrangements between a parent corporation and its insurance company subsidiary did not constitute insurance for federal income tax purposes. The court also held, however, that arrangements between the insurance company subsidiary and several dozen other subsidiaries of the parent (operating an even larger number of hospitals) qualified as insurance for federal income tax purposes because the requisite risk shifting and risk distribution were present. But see Malone & Hyde, Inc. v. Commissioner, 62 F.3d 835 (6th Cir. 1995) (concluding the lack of a business purpose, the undercapitalization of the offshore captive insurance subsidiary and the existence of related party guarantees established that the substance of the transaction did not support the taxpayer's characterization of the transaction as insurance). In Kidde Industries, Inc. v. United States, 40 Fed. Cl. 42 (1997), the United States Court of Federal Claims concluded that an arrangement between the captive insurance subsidiary and each of the 100 operating subsidiaries of the same parent constituted insurance for federal income tax purposes. As in Humana, the insurer in Kidde insured only entities within its affiliated group during the taxable years at issue.

In the present case, the professional liability risks of 12 operating subsidiaries are shifted to *S*. Further, the premiums of the operating subsidiaries, determined at arms-length, are pooled such that a loss by one operating subsidiary is borne, in substantial part, by the premiums paid by others. The 12 operating subsidiaries and *S* conduct themselves in all respects as would unrelated parties to a traditional insurance relationship, and *S* is regulated as an insurance company in each state where it does business. The narrow question presented is whether *P's* common ownership of the 12 operating subsidiaries and *S* affects the conclusion that the arrangements at issue are insurance for federal income tax purposes. Under the facts presented, we conclude the arrangements between *S* and each of the 12 operating subsidiaries of *S's* parent constitute insurance for federal income tax purposes.

HOLDING

The amounts paid for professional liability coverage by the 12 domestic operating subsidiaries to *S* are "insurance premiums" deductible under § 162.

EFFECT ON OTHER DOCUMENTS

Rev. Rul. 2001–31, 2001–1 C.B. 1348, is amplified.

* * *